EMBRACING
THE ADOPTION EFFECT

Also by Barbara Taylor Blomquist

Insight Into Adoption
Randy's Ride
Searching for Abby

BARBARA TAYLOR BLOMQUIST

EMBRACING THE ADOPTION EFFECT

29 STORIES OF FAMILIES TOUCHED BY ADOPTION

TATE PUBLISHING
AND ENTERPRISES, LLC

Embracing the Adoption Effect
Copyright © 2015 by Barbara Taylor Blomquist. All rights reserved.

No part of this publication may be reproduced, stored in a retrieval system or transmitted in any way by any means, electronic, mechanical, photocopy, recording or otherwise without the prior permission of the author except as provided by USA copyright law.

This book is designed to provide accurate and authoritative information with regard to the subject matter covered. This information is given with the understanding that neither the author nor Tate Publishing, LLC is engaged in rendering legal, professional advice. Since the details of your situation are fact dependent, you should additionally seek the services of a competent professional.

The opinions expressed by the author are not necessarily those of Tate Publishing, LLC.

Published by Tate Publishing & Enterprises, LLC
127 E. Trade Center Terrace | Mustang, Oklahoma 73064 USA
1.888.361.9473 | www.tatepublishing.com

Tate Publishing is committed to excellence in the publishing industry. The company reflects the philosophy established by the founders, based on Psalm 68:11,
"The Lord gave the word and great was the company of those who published it."

Book design copyright © 2015 by Tate Publishing, LLC. All rights reserved.
Cover design by Jeffrey Doblados
Interior design by Mary Jean Archival

Published in the United States of America

ISBN: 978-1-68118-563-7
Family & Relationships / Adoption & Fostering
15.05.22

Contents

Prologue 7

Section I

1 The Interviews 13
2 Adoptive-Parent Perspective 19
3 Birth-Parent Perspective 23
4 Adoptee Perspective 27
5 The Searching Group 31
6 The Search 37

Section II

7 The Adoptee 43
8 Adoptee Profiles 47

Section III

9 Birth Parents 77
10 Birth-Parent Profiles 81

Section IV

11　Adoptive Parents 107
12　Adoptive-Parent Profiles 111

Section V

13　Loss and Gain 157
14　Adoptee Loss and Gain 159
15　Birth-Parent Loss and Gain 167
16　Adoptive-Parent Loss and Gain 175
17　Adoptive Families 185
18　Perspective 193

Prologue

This is a book filled with stories. The people in these stories are real. This book is the result of many hours of interviews with people whose lives have been touched and altered by adoption. Their names and some circumstances and details have been modified to protect their privacy. Many of these stories have been buried and hidden for years because they often started with a secret: the secret of a birth.

A few years ago, two adoption social workers and I started a project of interviewing all three sides of the adoption triad (adoptee, birth parents, and adoptive parents) with the goal of writing a book that would unite the triad by helping them understand one another. That book was never written.

These stories lay dormant for four years, but these stories and the voices that told them need to be heard. They are powerful stories showing the strength of the human spirit. The stories are unique and still they are not, for many involved in the adoption world have had similar experiences. The stories of these lives say so much about the people who lived them.

The people portrayed in these pages were involved in the adoption process primarily in the 1960s, 1970s, and 1980s, so we were talking only with adults. They'd had some years to develop a perspective on their experiences.

As interviewers, we were impressed with the strength of the people we interviewed. Many endured years of sadness, unfairness, and much more. Much of it was their own reaction to adoption, but much of it was inflicted upon them by society. In the end, however, they all survived, and an impressive number climbed to the top of their own almost insurmountable mountain to be triumphant.

We are grateful to all members of the adoption triad who participated in our interviewing process. We thanked them profusely for being open and honest about how adoption has affected their lives. They, in turn, thanked us for allowing them hours of freedom to talk candidly about how they felt. The safe environment of the interviews and the purpose of the interviews allowed them to speak openly, sadly, often for the very first time. The challenge of a situation is sometimes alleviated if it is talked about honestly and shared with others. We sensed this in our interviews.

Their hope was that their story might let people know of—and, better yet, understand—the effect of adoption on their lives. They told us that in the past they had stopped talking about their adoption experience because people discounted it as not being important.

Everyone has been impacted by circumstances in their lives, but in the adoption world, there has been secrecy and denial and ignorance about many of the repercussions, which can last for years, stretching out to lifetimes.

The purpose of this book is to share these stories so that the reader might find a common connection with the storytellers. For those personally involved in the adoption world, they have the opportunity of seeing themselves in some stories and hearing about the impact on the other two sides of the triad. For those not involved directly with adoption, hopefully these stories will show that adoption is a real issue. It is deep, lifelong, and it has an effect. A good way to test this is to ask how the stories told here might have been different if adoption had not been a part of their lives.

During the interviews, we witnessed anger, resentment, sadness, and tears, as well as compassion, tenacity, forgiveness, tolerance, strength of character, love, and great joy. People are noble, and they are also very human. The people on the following pages are remarkable.

Thank you to the following who graciously shared their stories: Marilyn, Pat, Bob, Sue, Jennifer, Ann, Ted, Tom, Glen, Marne, John, Mary, David, Beverly, Carol, Linda, Rich, Bruce, Mike, Michelle, Amy, Dennis, Terry, Gene, Katie, Brooke, Don, Leonard, Margaret, Beth, Maria, Eric, Peggy, and Molly.

Because the loss factor was not recognized as real, these adoptees, birth parents, and adoptive parents learned to hide their role in adoption, all the while needing help in understanding their situation and seeing only empty space where that help should have been. Many were judged by people who thought adoptees, birth parents, and adoptive parents were just not very adequate people and caused their own problems. All three sides of the triad were misunderstood, bringing them to sometimes think that maybe, indeed, they did cause their own problems. With no support available, some internalized the blame and lived with a feeling of being inadequate. Now we know better, and there is recognition of the effects of loss on the human soul.

These stories range from tales of survivorship to tales of nobility. Their internal struggles were clear to the interviewers, and knowing everyone did the best they were equipped to do, even those who merely survived impressed us as we saw the depth of their burden and their struggle to either live with it or overcome it.

SECTION I

1

The Interviews

The adoption effect – many people think there is no adoption effect. Even some adoptees and adoptive parents want to believe there is no adoption effect. The following stories may shed some light on the answer.

This is mainly a book of stories, stories about people's lives. The stories are about people who chose to adopt children, people who gave birth to children they did not raise, and people who had no say in their adoption. In some instances, there were choices, and in other instances, there were no choices. These three factions—the adoptee, the adoptive parents, and the birth parents—collectively make up each and every single adoption. This act has a lifelong immeasurable effect on all of them.

Embracing the Adoption Effect is a work based upon a series of interviews with these three factions. A few years back, two social workers asked me to join them in writing a book about the adoption triad. We interviewed people from the three sides: birth parent, adoptee, and adoptive parent. That book never was written, but the interviews done in preparation for that book should be acknowledged. These people had stories to tell. We didn't interview a large-enough number to come to any statistical conclusions, but it was large enough for us to see a pattern. The lives of all those whom we spoke with were affected by adoption, some favorably and some unfavorably.

It turned out that the most obvious thread pervading all the interviews had nothing to do with adoption. It was not what their circumstances were. It was their *attitude toward their circumstances* that directed their life! People who saw themselves as victims of the adoption system had a hard life. Those who were grateful for their lives and had a generous spirit toward others fared very well.

Each person and each family comes from its own genetic background. They interact and react differently from one another. We all have emotional baggage we collect throughout our lives. Some people can handle life better than others. Sometimes we think we've put an episode behind us until the middle of some night when we awaken and ponder why a certain thing happened to us. We wonder why we can't get over feeling a certain way. We try to get back to sleep, but that nagging thought of being hurt or insulted or treated unfairly won't let go of us. We act and react to instances in life while we're carrying around this baggage, which can make us at times illogical, overly sensitive, and reactive.

Facing reality, adoptive parents are no more or less perfect than biological parents. Adopted children are no more or less perfect than biological children. If we breathe air, we are alive, and if we are alive, we all have a variety of life experiences which form us.

These stories portray a slice of humanity. Some tales are sad, some tragic, some uplifting, some heroic, but they are, in the end, just stories of how people cope with their lives, more specifically of how they cope with the hand life has dealt them. None of us has a choice about that, but we do have a choice as to how we handle our circumstances.

If there is a common thread, a common lesson in all of this, it's that some of us do better at seeing the bright side of life than others. As you'll see from the following stories, some have been dealt very,

very difficult hands but come up smiling and successful because they know they've done their very best. Maybe they couldn't turn all of the bad things in their lives into good things, but they saw the best in themselves and others, and that's where they spent their lives. Others who might even have been dealt easier hands allowed the small negative things to take over their thinking and their lives. They complained about the unfairness of life and particularly their own lot in life. Their lives reflect their negative attitude.

We could divide the people into winners and whiners. The winners believed they had a successful life because they dealt with their circumstances the very best way they could. It didn't matter if the hand life dealt them was easy or hard. That was never, ever the point. The point in their being satisfied and pleased with success, as they saw it, was that they handled their circumstances well.

Everything we experience has an effect on our lives. However, the way we filter our experiences in our minds can vary from person to person. We've all experienced something along with another person and learned that the impressions left behind can be individualized. I had the experience one time of listening to a friend tell a story to a group, and we were all on the edges of our seats, waiting for the drama to unfold. It took me a few minutes to realize I'd experienced that episode along with that person. My version was very different from the one I was hearing my friend relate. Mine was calmer and duller.

In the following interviews, we were looking for a common thread from the adoption experience that united all three sides of the adoption triad. The thought was to somehow unify the adoption world so it would be less fragmented. It appeared all too often that adoptees were angry at their birth parents for relinquishing them, birth parents were resentful that they were 'forced' to give up their child, and adoptive parents were tentative and fearful that their child would want to return to his or her birth family if they were ever to be found. There was surface cooperation among the triad, as it is called, but there was often underlying animosity as well.

During this interviewing process, we became fascinated with how one's attitude colored one's experiences. In the following stories, I'll state the facts as given by the person interviewed, and the reader can determine how adoption and attitude affected the individual's life.

The world outside adoption has a tendency to see those affected by adoption as living in a world apart from theirs, thinking that they are "normal" and people in the adoption world are not. Too often, those in the adoption triad have bought this and accepted this thinking. The adopted child may be thought of as different from the biological child. The adoptive parents aren't 'true' parents, and the birth parent years ago was relegated to a world with no comparison. Even as adults, there are some participants who still see themselves as scarred by adoption. This need not be.

The hope is that somewhere in this book, the adoptee, adoptive parent, or birth parent will recognize kindred souls who feel and think the same way they do. All feelings are legitimate, but we have a choice of how we handle those feelings. In delving into the adoption world, one will find that many adoptees, birth parents, and adoptive parents think their thoughts are so different from others that they sometimes feel abnormal. They are not. They have logical feelings stemming from logical facts. However, if these facts can be viewed objectively, perhaps the light that has been shone on them will provide warm understanding.

We are all human, often put into circumstances in life that we didn't choose for ourselves. We have a right to react to perceived rejection, insecurity, etc., but we shouldn't have to let these facts affect us negatively. *It's time to see them for what they are.* They don't need to be a part of our persona. We have a choice. This is shown in the interviews. Some people carried this negativity like a stone on their shoulders while others used the perceived negative fact to grow stronger and establish a better life.

These attitude choices can be seen throughout the following stories. For example, the difference attitude makes was obvious with some birth parents. The loss of their baby was the common fact. Some said it ruined their life, they couldn't maintain a relationship after that; they hated and resented the adoptive parents who stole "their" child. The next birth mother we interviewed would say giving up her baby to a loving family with two parents was the blessing of her life. She was grateful that her child would be happy and healthy, and have opportunities she couldn't have provided. The facts were the same, but there were two very different perspectives. We found this over and over. It wasn't the facts that made a person happy or unhappy; it was their attitude toward the facts. Their attitude dictated how they perceived each and every issue they faced.

Playing the what-if game is usually not a good idea. At other times, it helps to bring perspective to a situation. In the adoption process, all decisions are made by people. All these decisions have lifelong implications, some positive and some negative, depending on your outlook.

In reading the following stories, it's interesting to ask "What if?" What if the birth mothers had kept their babies? How different would the adoptee's life be if they had been raised by their birth family? What if the adoptive parents had never adopted their children? What if the adoption agency had placed their child into a different adoptive home? What if the adoption agency had given the adoptive parents a different child?

How would their lives have been changed? Would they have been easier or harder, more or less satisfying? And finally, what effect did adoption have on the people involved? More importantly, how did these effects influence their lives? And lastly, did they have a choice in how the effects of adoption shaped their lives?

The stories included here will speak for themselves.

2

Adoptive-Parent Perspective

It's natural that adoptive parents can be overly sensitive to their own personal parent/child relationship. They know it is unique and something that is man-made versus nature made. Human decisions were part of the equation regarding the placement of their child into their family. In a biological family, nature takes care of all that. Parents and social workers and adoption agencies don't make decisions about a child's placement in their situation. It is accepted as it is. No questions asked.

For an adoptive parent, it can seem that no one understands just how unique your family is. You are raising children who have no genetic link to you or your spouse. For most of the time, that is of no importance or relevance at all. However, throughout the many years of family life, there are times when it can have a great impact on your family.

We all know that most people we meet think that adoptive issues are not very valid. They say, "Oh, my children aren't adopted, and we have the same situation in our family." We as adoptive parents know that it is not the same situation. It may look similar on the outside, but the motivation of the child could be quite different because the adopted child does not always react to situations the same way that a biological child would. Their background is different in that they are connected to their families in a different way. When life gets difficult in adoptive families, the child can reexamine that tie and feel less secure than a biological child might in the same set of circumstances.

From the adoptive parents' point of view, problems can occur if they look upon their children as extensions of themselves rather than as the unique individuals they actually are. Many adoptive parents spend years trying to mold their adopted children so they will "fit" into their family. In our interviews, we heard over and over that adoptees feel this pressure to conform in order to be accepted by the adoptive family. Adoptive parents' expectations could be unrealistic, and many adoptees feel they could not be true to their own innate identity because of this pressure.

Instead, adoptive parents should realize they have a rare opportunity to nurture and cherish a human being born to strangers. What a gift from life! The wonder of it all is that certain adoptive parents were destined by a myriad of circumstances to be the home where a particular child lands to start his or her life. What a responsibility – and privilege.

Consistently, throughout our interviews with adoptive parents, we were surprised again and again when adoptive parents who had spent hours relating how difficult their family life had been stated they would go through it all again. They said there were two reasons for this. The first is that they loved their child and could not conceive of anyone else parenting "their" child. The second reason was that they felt they came through it all a better person. They said they would not want to go back to being the person they had been before. Their eyes had been opened to the broad spectrum of humanity that affects some lives. They acquired an understanding and, more than that, an appreciation for life they never would have had without adoption in their lives. They viewed all of life in a different way. They were grateful for their child, the opportunity to discover their higher inner selves, and the awe factor in life. They said they felt they were one of the fortunate few touched by adoption.

3

Birth-Parent Perspective

It's important to remember the history surrounding the attitude regarding babies born out of wedlock. The atmosphere surrounding this is very different now than in years past. Up until the 1960s, in the United States this was a very dramatic event, with the people involved being judged harshly by society. The young woman and young man responsible, as well as the families of the unwed parents, did not want to be disparaged by others. This led to secrecy and fictitious stories, such as that the young lady, during her pregnancy, was away at school, visiting an aunt, had moved to another city to find a job, etc. She would usually return to her hometown six to eight months later, slimmed down and without any baby. Often her education was curtailed in this process. Many in this situation say they felt their normal life had been destroyed. They went on to live years and years carrying their "shameful" secret.

Many adult adoptees today were the result of this system. Most of the birth parents we interviewed spoke from this experience. Many birth mothers who gave birth during this time are still ashamed of their unplanned pregnancy and are still secretive about it. It is not unusual for a husband and subsequent children to have no knowledge of any prior birth.

In our interviews, many birth parents stated they wanted to keep their babies, but their parents were adamant that they did not want that shame attached to their family. There was also the issue of the child being stigmatized if people knew he was born out of wedlock. So for years, for many reasons logical at the time, almost all babies born out of wedlock were placed for adoption.

It was felt that it was a win-win situation. The baby would have a loving two-parent home, the birth mother could get on with her life, and the adoptive parents would raise a child they could not produce themselves. It turned out not to be that simple. All three sides of the triad had issues that, in some cases, were not too severe and handled reasonably. However, in many families, unspoken issues proved to be devastating to family harmony.

It seemed to be a general rule that each and every birth parent we spoke to said that once their child had been adopted and they were back again in the family fold, the event of the pregnancy was never spoken of again. Their family's attitude was one of denial. The pain and guilt felt by the young birth parent was never addressed, and in many cases, it was the basis for part of their self-identity from that point on. They covered up their "shameful" past. Some women who married later on stated they married a man they didn't love and didn't even like that much, but that was what they felt they deserved because no decent man would marry a tarnished woman. Some married the birth father years later when they were both in their twenties, but a higher percent than in the normal population never married at all.

Birth mothers who gave birth and relinquished their baby in those days say they still live with "a hole in my heart." The grief and pain over the years often turned to a feeling of loss and emptiness. After giving birth, most were told they were "bad" girls, and now they had to go back home, forget about what they had done, and get on with their lives. They could not forget, so they felt there was something wrong with them. They were alone with their unresolved grief.

Birth fathers, in years past, were not too involved in the relinquishment process because prior to the 1980s, it was not necessary for the pregnant woman to name the father. If the birth mother was sent away to have her baby, often the birth father never knew he was about to become a father. In some cases, he learned after everything was all settled, or in many cases, he never was told at all. If birth fathers were told, it was more common that they, being young and scared, could not and did not want to take responsibility. Because of this system, the birth mother would provide information to the adoption agency about her family, but little was provided about the father's side.

Years ago, when the birth father did not need to be identified, he was not part of the decision toward adoption. It fell on the birth mother and her family to make decisions. This proved to be very frustrating and painful for young men who thought of this action as an affront against their manhood, even though most were teens at the time. Many years later, in our interviews, they expressed how they carried this pain for years, more often than not still carrying a picture of their newborn in their wallets. Some wanted to be a father to their child, but society at the time made a contrary decision, and they had no recourse.

4

Adoptee Perspective

It is almost too simple to say adoptees fall into two camps – the first being those who are disturbed on an ongoing basis that they were adopted and the second, others who are so happy with themselves, their adoptive families, and their lives that they say "Thank heavens I'm adopted." Life is not always this clear, however. There are many adoptees in between these two poles who vacillate between the two positions depending on what's going on in their lives.

Whether an adoptee is raised in a well-balanced, loving family or a dysfunctional family seems not to be the factor forming how he feels. We see adoptees who were placed in a very positive, supportive family yet seemed determined to disrupt their family's lives as well as their own. Conversely, sometimes an adoptee who was adopted by what turned out to be a dysfunctional family thought "Well, it might have been worse in my biological family." This difference in attitude and outlook on life is very personal and appears to be an innate attitude within each adoptee. Is the glass half-full or half-empty?

We all have met many adoptees who are very secure in their tie to their families. They see no need to search for a part of their past. To them, it is not at all relevant to their present life. Then there are adoptees who say that their counterparts who do not search are simply in denial. Some adoptees think that every adoptee must want to know their biological beginnings. They think that those who don't search are in some way traitors to the cause of searching because they won't acknowledge it's important to them.

The conclusion could be made that searchers are more distressed with their lives than nonsearchers. It appears that there is dissatisfaction within their lives. They appear to be discontent and are searching to find the missing part of their own personal puzzle. In the following interviews, where a search was implemented and successful, most of the people involved are very happy with the results. Most said they are now whole. Even when the people found were not as expected, the search provided an ending, an answer to their wondering.

Nonsearchers say they don't need any more information to make them whole. And, indeed, they do appear to be happier. One doesn't see evidence of any internal struggle regarding their identity issues. Is it buried so deeply that not even the adoptee knows it's there, or perhaps it does not exist at all in their psyche?

There are many wise people who say our past is our past. Let it be. In working with those who are searching and those who are not, it is very obvious that the searching think they will not be complete until they find their link to their biological background. They need to know their past. Nonsearchers take the attitude that they are who they are. They are in control of their lives, and it makes little or no difference what their biological origin was. They appear to be content within themselves and what they have done with their lives.

Many of these nonsearching adoptees have good families and childhoods, but that is not the criteria for searching. It seems to be an attitude that divides the two groups, not their family experiences.

The searchers take the attitude that they are a link in a line of people and they need to know what line they came from. Nonsearchers take the attitude that they are a unique person and part of a universal "personhood." To them, the biological origin is no more than a vehicle in becoming a human being. Once here, they are a free person, able to structure their lives as they see fit. They are not bogged down by their past (or lack of past) and appear to live much freer and less stressful lives.

The conclusion could be that we live our lives according to our attitudes. With one attitude, we can be content, and with another attitude, we are not content. Do we have a choice? Wise men would say that we do. Is it easy to change our attitude? Some would say not. We always have a choice, but some adoptees find it almost impossible to let go of the past. It haunts them and affects them on a daily basis. Adoptive parents all too often just have to live with this fact.

5

The Searching Group

It's amazing the impact that one phone call can have. My phone rang at about ten o'clock on a Monday morning in June 2004. The voice on the other end identified herself as being from the adoption agency where we adopted our two sons.

"Your son's birth mother has written a letter and would like to get it to your son, but we couldn't locate him," she said. "Obviously, we were able to locate you. Can you give us your son's phone number?"

"Which son?" I asked, hoping in my heart that it was the son who, at one period in his life, wanted contact with his birth mother. At that dramatic moment, I didn't realize that this phone call was a real-life example of what I had been exposed to in a support group I'd attended every month for several years.

Four years previously, a friend of mine told me about a support group of searchers composed of birth parents searching for the children they had relinquished decades ago and adult adoptees searching for their birth parents. My friend said they wanted the whole triad in this group but found it difficult to get adoptive parents to attend.

That was certainly understandable to me, and would be to any adoptive parent! What adoptive parent would go to a meeting where children are trying to connect with the parents who gave birth to them but don't even know them? We adoptive parents are the ones who have been in the trenches all these years; we're the ones who loved our children through all the sleepless nights, frustrating parental experiences, and joys our children have afforded us.

Through the years in this support group, I have indeed been the sole, consistent voice for adoptive parenting. Another adoptive parent may show up once a year, but they never came back a second time because the conversation is painful to hear.

I kept going back because the voice of the adoptive parent was needed—not always, but upon occasion. It was needed on those occasions when an adoptee would proclaim "I don't know why my adoptive mother was so upset when I spent last Mother's Day with my birth mother and not with her" or "I don't know why my parents think I'm going to spend time and holidays with my birth parent instead of with them."

It was at times like those that I could interject and try to explain the ultimate fear of all adoptive parents: the fear that our children will leave us for another, original set of parents. I was constantly amazed that the adoptees were always surprised by my remark. Unanimously they told me that they couldn't see how this could happen. They say they only have one set of parents, that their adoptive parents are their only parents and always will be. This statement came from adoptees who were searching for their birth parents at the time.

In actuality, the sessions were not so much about the mechanics of searching for a birth child or a birth parent (although that certainly was an important point of discussion for them), but it was discussing the adoption issues that surfaced after many years of suppression or denial. The anger, frustration, sense of aloneness, sense of being different from the rest of the world—all these and many more were discussed by both birth parents and adoptees because these elements belonged to both of them. This group provided a safe place to bring up these issues that they felt the rest of the world didn't understand.

Who among us doesn't want to belong? Who among us doesn't want to be loved, and who among us doesn't want to be remembered? I don't think there is anyone who doesn't want and need all these things. I have seen adoptees transformed and personalities changed to a degree after reunion with their birth parents (birth mothers in particular).

At these meetings, some adults now searching for their birth parents may seem sad to the world outside of adoption. Outsiders may be tempted to say "Why do you need that information? Why do you need to know? You're an adult now." There is a saying that once a mother, always a mother. In these meetings, I've learned how true that is, but I've also observed that in some cases, once a child, always a child.

Many adoptees I've grown to know well were desperate to find their birth mothers. They appeared to have a child's needs, needs that could only be satisfied by finding their birth mother. After the reunion, whether it was positive or negative, these adoptees emerged as whole adults. A missing piece of themselves had been put back in place, and now they were whole, like the rest of the world. This hardly ensured their happiness as often new issues that were difficult to handle came into their lives, but they did become whole through this experience. The missing piece of their puzzle had been replaced.

Previously, I had written a book about adoptive parenting, *Insight Into Adoption*, and in that book, I wrote that the almighty search has nothing to do with the adoptive parents. That was demonstrated over and over in these support meetings. Adoptees from wonderful, loving homes searched as well as adoptees who never felt they belonged in their adoptive homes. The need to find their personal missing part of their puzzle was their own individual unique drive. It had to do with personality.

There was one set of thirty-six-year-old twin women. One needed to search and the other didn't, but both had to agree in order to proceed with the search. They had been adopted into the same family, and both said they came from a particularly loving family with supportive parents. Even with all their commonalities, their needs were individualized.

And so it was that all this time I was attending these meetings to give a lone voice to the very lopsided adoption triangle, I didn't realize that I was being prepared to handle that phone call from our adoption agency. I certainly agree and respect the fact that most adoptive parents would not want to attend these meetings, but I feel that even though I went to offer the thoughts of an adoptive parent, while there, I learned much more than I ever taught. I gained the knowledge that some human beings, *if they feel the need*, have to know their history, their heritage, their beginnings.

Many adoptees are not one bit interested in searching for this, but I learned that other adoptees appear to be almost emotionally paralyzed because they don't have the biological part of their identity and heritage. As one adoptee said, "I'm not looking for a parent. I'm looking for me."

In one of these sessions, one adoptee made the statement "I don't want to be adopted, I want to be normal." For some, finding their birth roots makes them feel normal because they then feel they were born to people, just like everyone else. Often they learn names and places, which makes it real. Some need this step clarified to feel whole.

It is not always hugs and kisses, as is shown on TV these days when reunions are televised. Often, one need is satisfied by reuniting, but many other issues are introduced into the adoptee's life and the birth parent's life. Obviously, this has a large effect on the adoptive family and their lives; in fact, it can change the dynamics of the family. The important thing I learned, however, is that the need to search is not affected one way or the other by the quality, or lack of quality, of the adoptive family. The need to search is a need within a person. This need is hardly universal, but if a person has the need to search for a birth parent—or a birth parent for a child—the search can, to a degree, take over their lives. Like so many other "needs," it can mesmerize them until the need is met.

Another lesson I learned from this group is that adopted children/adults only talk in terms of one set of parents: their adoptive parents. Many conversations start with "When I say 'parents,' of course I mean my adoptive parents." The sad irony of this is that adoptive parents think they may lose their children when children search for birth parents, not knowing that adoptees consider they only have one set of parents. Adoptees are appalled their parents would think otherwise. They say they are searching for people, not parents!

The strongest lesson I learned is that for some adoptees, that "obvious" tie to their adoptive parents is not felt in a reciprocal way. In these sessions, I heard over and over again verbiage indicating that these adoptees did not feel like real children in real families. There was often that phantom, usually unspoken feeling of not fitting in, not being a true child to a true parent.

To anyone attending these meetings, the loud message going out to all adoptive parents is the imperative need for adoptive parents to tell and show their adopted children how strong and permanent and unconditional their love is. Adopted children need to hear they will always belong and be loved unconditionally. They need that in words and actions – over and over again. Many adoptive parents think their actions will prove it. Not so. We need to tell our children in words and prove it to them every day. Many adopted children truly don't know. They don't or can't feel it. They grow up immersed in their own attitude of feeling different, and because of that difference, they think they don't truly belong in our families. They can show it through negative behavior, but adoptive parents don't see this as a signal to further cement our bonds with our children. We see it as merely "acting out."

Adoptive parents need to be vigilant and vocal in convincing their children that they will always be their children. Adopted children hope they only have one set of parents and adoptive parents only have one kind of child—the permanent kind! Both sides feel it from their own viewpoint, but too many don't know if the other half of the relationship feels the same way.

The most shocking statement I heard from adult adoptees in the support group was, when asked if they felt their adoptive parents loved them, some answered, "Sure, they love me—you know, as much as adoptive parents can love an adopted child." This would break the heart of any adoptive parent.

6

The Search

"The Search." A powerful concept is created when these six letters are put together and prefaced by the word *the*. "The Search" conjures up the deepest of human emotions. Even though adoptees, adoptive parents, and birth parents are all deeply affected by the search, each thinks of it very, very differently. When a group is together and talking about adoption, if the search is mentioned in conversation, no one needs to ask, "Searching for what?" Everyone knows, and emotions are immediately high.

When a search results in a reunion, it sometimes happens that the only tie the adoptee and birth parent have with each other is a blood tie. They are strangers trying to forge a connection. The timing of any reunion is shown to be crucial. One party may be ready, but that doesn't mean the other is. After a reunion, whether the two sides meet personally or just over the phone, one party may want to slow down to absorb what is going on while the other party may want to go ahead vigorously to get to know each other. This can cause some problems.

The adoptee probably has the most mixed emotions, starting with an excitement that he/she may find the parents who gave birth to him as well as finding aunts, uncles, cousins, grandparents, and, very importantly, sisters and/or brothers. This excitement can be followed by fear that his original family may not want to be found or, if found, may not accept him as a part of their family. The worst scenario the adoptee can imagine is denial that he was born. Some attempted reunions have resulted in the adoptee being told "I never gave birth to a baby on that date. I'm not your mother, and don't bother me again." The thought of this potential rejection, although not very common, is often enough to stop the adoptee from searching. The adoptee's emotions can run the gamut from exhilaration to despair.

The birth parent's feelings usually depend on their current circumstances in life, as well as how they have adjusted to giving up their child. Some think about it often, hoping one day to be reunited. Others have forcefully put it far back in their minds and don't want to bring it out into the light again.

Some have been waiting every day for the phone to ring and a voice on the other end to say "I think you're my birth mother." They are hoping for the opportunity to reunite and tell their birth child that they truly did not want to put them into the adoption system. Life at that time was beyond their control, and they had no choice—no choice at all. Other birth parents have closed their minds to the child they have given birth to. They don't want to reopen that part of their life. Often the child can be representative of a negative traumatic situation in their past.

In both situations, those who want to reunite and those who do not, informing the birth parent's current family that another child exists, can be the issue stopping the reunion. At the time of contact, the birth parent can find it very difficult to inform their spouse (if they have not already done so) and particularly difficult to inform any children born to them after the child they relinquished for adoption. A trust factor surfaces here, and the logical question from the family is "What else in your past haven't you told us about?"

For the adoptive parents, the emotions are just as deep, but they are more universal than with the others in the triad. Their main fear is that their child will leave them, physically or psychologically, to go to their birth family. Even though all parents want what is best for their child (and a reunion may or may not be), certainly one of the worst thoughts all adoptive parents have is that their child will leave them.

One woman in an adoptive-parent support group stated, "I know I'll have my child until he is eighteen, and then he'll probably want to go to his birth family. At least I'll have him for eighteen years." This is not a common thought among adoptive parents, but the seed is there. They know their child is also attached in some unseen way to another set of parents.

This book explores all the emotions involved among all three sides of the adoption triad. There are as many differences as there are people. We are, after all, unique individuals, and we react uniquely within our own lives. Exploring those lives is very revealing and educational.

There are many examples of lives that are working well. There are also examples of lives that are bogged down by adoption issues of one kind or another. There is logic to everyone's story and justification for their handling of their lives. There is no point in being judgmental because individual reactions and feelings are real and valid to each individual in their own unique situation. The fact that some individuals seem to live happier, more productive lives speaks for itself. Perhaps there is a lesson to be learned, a perspective to be gained. The reader can determine for himself.

SECTION II

7

The Adoptee

The adoptee, of course, is the pivotal person in the adoption triad. The birth parents and the adoptive parents make conscious decisions to enter into the adoption world. The adoptee, on the contrary, has no say in this.

Below is a short summation of the type of interview questions we asked adoptees:

- How and when did you learn you were adopted?
- How did your adoptive parents refer to your birth parents, positively or negatively? Did they show you legal papers, have biological information for you? How much could they tell you?
- What was their attitude toward your birth parents? What was your attitude toward your birth parents?
- Did your parents have other adopted children, biological children? Where were you in the birth order?

- How did/do you feel about your siblings? Biological or also adopted?
- Have you thought about searching for your birth parents? Have you acted on this? How have you done this? How does this make you feel? Do your adoptive parents know, or have you kept this secret from them? If they know, do they support you? What is their attitude?
- If you have had a reunion with your birth parents, was it successful? Explain the different phases.
- If you found any birth relatives, what has been your reaction? Your adoptive parents' reaction? Any sibling reaction?
- Has your relationship with your adoptive parents changed if you now have a relationship with birth relatives? How?
- What was the reaction of the "found" birth relatives? What is the relationship like now?
- How has this changed your self-image?
- How do you see this new relationship affecting your life in the future?
- Do you feel you were raised as a unique individual, or did your parents try to mold you so you would be "one of them"? Do you think you were treated differently than their biological child would have been?
- How did your adoptive parents' attitude affect your task of growing up? Did you feel like you truly were their child, that you belonged?
- Hindsight: if given the choice, would you have preferred to have been raised by your birth family or your adoptive family?
- How would you describe your relationship with your adoptive parents now that you are an adult?

This is a brief outline of some of our questions, and because almost all of the questions are open-ended, the discussions were long and deep. Many adoptees said they'd never told anybody before how they felt about these issues, which were so personal to them. Sadly, they said no one had ever asked.

From the profiles that follow, one can see a range of reactions among those who have the status of being an adoptee.

8

Adoptee Profiles

Terry Jordan, Adoptee

The search and reunion process in adoption can be analogous to a train trip. One gets on a train with anticipation and a feeling of adventure. Beginning an adoption search is similar. There is anticipation and a feeling of going to a place where you've never been before, knowing the experience will change your life in one way or another.

During a train trip, each time the train stops at a station, people get on and off. Comparing a search journey to a train journey, at each stop in a search, everyone who climbs aboard is related to you. You continue on your journey, but you have added more people in your group. Perhaps if there are other birth family members to meet, you can compare it to stopping at additional stations along the track, and each time, more people are added to your group. At each stop, people greet and hug each other, and then you can almost imagine them mentally deciding how to sit in the train. Who sits closest to the adoptee, who are the critical players in the reunion, and who are the family members who are on the fringe of the dynamics? You can imagine the possible awkwardness involved.

At the beginning of this hypothetical trip, the searcher is alone. After the first stop to pick up one family member, perhaps more, a whole new dynamics is born. People, who are now adults and have had a family status that has been stable for years, must now adjust to a different picture of family dynamics. The dynamics of the relationships can change each time another person is added to the picture. Not everyone will agree as to just where they or where other family members should fit. Normal stress and tension can result.

Some searchers are at the beginning of this journey, some have just stopped at the first station, and others are way down the track with the adjusting and readjusting well under way.

Terry is an example of an adoptee who is so far down the track that he is almost out of sight. At age twenty-four, he started to think about searching because he had always felt so different from other members of his family. It wasn't until ten years later, however, that Terry made the search and found his biological family. He said that at age twenty-four, he wouldn't have been ready emotionally for the reunion because he still was working with indiscriminate anger issues as well as with issues surrounding his concept of his own identity. Terry added that he couldn't imagine himself dealing with an open adoption. He said the identity confusion rising from that must be very confusing to a young child, perhaps overwhelming at times.

Three years ago, Terry was reunited with his birth mother, his birth sister, and then his birth father. He learned that his birth parents married each other five years after Terry was born, and five years after that, his sister was born. Their marriage ended in divorce after fifteen years.

Terry's search and reunion would be called a success. However, Terry has worked intensely, with the help of an excellent therapist, to sort out the dynamics of incorporating his newly found birth family into his life, which already was comprised of his adoptive parents and two brothers (also adopted). Many times this was a struggle for Terry because he was sensitive enough to want to take this personal journey of his without hurting anyone along the way.

At first, he felt pulled in different directions by the two families. Terry felt a commitment to them both, and it took a toll on him because he was trying to be a "good son" to both families. Both families live in the same city, and holidays particularly were stressful.

After three years of adjusting to his new role of son in not just one but now two families, Terry said, "I can see very clearly that if an adoptee isn't squared away emotionally and psychologically, he or she could really fall apart with the stress of all this. You get your biological identity by finding your biological family, but you as a person can really become fragmented trying to be all things to both families. You can lose your own sense of self along the way. I don't think I could have done it successfully without some professional help."

Within Terry's adoptive family, there was tension after his reunion because they felt the natural threat that Terry would find more of a sense of belonging within his biological family. Terry worked very hard to dispel this. Now Terry feels close to both of his families, and most of the tension has dissipated as his adoptive family realizes he is still their son.

However, Terry always did feel different in his adoptive family, like he didn't fit. This is a very common feeling. He feels close to them because he has a history; actually, his whole history is with his adoptive parents and brothers. This is his "home." He also feels a closeness to his biological parents and sister because he can see himself in them. There is a familiarity among them in their temperaments, love of the arts, and intellectualism. These qualities were not shared within his adoptive family.

"I see some of my personality traits in my biological family," Terry said. "The funny thing is, some I like and some I don't like. I wasn't aware of these traits in me until I saw them in my birth parents and birth sister. It's funny how you can see something in someone else and not in yourself. It's given me the insight to change some of my behaviors. In a way, they have been like mirrors to me. I see myself in them."

When asked how the reunion has affected his view of himself as an adoptee, Terry replied, "I think of myself as adopted even more now than before, because I realize the impact that adoption had on my life. The two main issues I still deal with are lack of self-esteem and the fear of abandonment. I can now think of myself as Terry and not *adoptee* Terry because I've worked through my identity issues, but I do see more clearly now the impact of adoption on the adoptee."

Terry has learned that his identity includes being a part of two families. He says he doesn't wholly belong to either family. Terry diligently works very hard trying to keep a balance of trying to be an integral part of both. Over the past three years, Terry said he's learned that although he was the central figure in the search and reunion, staying in that role eventually tore him apart emotionally. He now sees that everyone in the two family dynamics has a responsibility to make the relationships viable and workable. The pressure of being the *good son* has been alleviated somewhat because Terry saw that he alone couldn't hold everything together.

"I try to be loving in all my relationships, but I am not responsible for how other people perceive my actions," he said. "It is no longer my responsibility to make sure that everyone in both my families is happy with my new situation. I've done a lot of soul-searching and have dealt with a lot of issues to come through this, but I can't do that same work for all of them. They need to work at this too."

Terry went on to say, "I think the success of the search is not the reunion but the opportunity the reunion affords you to be introspective about yourself and your identity. It allows you to grow as a person."

Terry also expressed the fact that he is realistic now about his adoption, that everyone in life is dealt something they have to deal with, and his issue is adoption. He could have been kept by his birth mother or put into another adoptive family other than his own, but he wasn't. This is what his life is; this is what he deals with.

He said he feels stronger as a person than he perhaps might have been had he not had to face this identity issue for so many years. Terry appears to be drawn to people who have had similar struggles in their lives because he thinks some experiences afford you the opportunity to learn and grow, and this can make you a deeper, stronger, more empathetic person. Terry's adoption has given him this opportunity, and he sees that very clearly now. He has indeed, through years of committed effort, come to terms with his adoption and himself even though he is realistic enough to say that he will be working on this his whole life.

Nick Camden, Adoptee

Nick – adoptee
Jane – his birth mother

For some searchers—adoptees, in particular—the whole process of wondering, searching, and reuniting turns out to be a vehicle for self-analysis. Nick was in his middle twenties when he went to the adoption agency that placed him. He asked if his birth mother had been looking for him. After being told that the agency had had no contact with her since his birth, Nick took this as a very personal rejection, the second time around. He had fantasized for years that his birth mother would reappear to rescue him. Now that his fantasy was over, he felt no one cared about him.

His life was not smooth during this time, and this news was devastating to him. For years, this second rejection just solidified his impression of himself that he was not a worthy person. Nick said he sought out other "unworthy" people because that was where he felt his life was to be lived. His birth parents and his adoptive parents had all attended college. Nick did not because he thought he wasn't college material. He dated girls he didn't respect but thought that was what he deserved. He had a short-lived failed marriage. In looking back, Nick says it should never have been. It was another bad choice.

While Nick was in his late twenties, his adoptive mother died. Nick said going through the funeral process was particularly hard because he thought people were judging him. Was he sorrowful enough, was he upset enough about his mother's death, did he overreact to her death? He thought he couldn't be himself and couldn't express himself honestly because he felt, first and foremost, that people were looking at him as the adopted son. His adopted sister cried a lot during the service, and Nick wondered if the tears were real or if she was acting like she thought she should act. In the support group the evening Nick told us about this experience, two other adoptees who had lost adoptive parents within the last year nodded and agreed with Nick. They told him they went through the same experience. They didn't know what was appropriate and said they never felt their adopted status more keenly.

In his midthirties, Nick tried to search again through a professional searcher and was this time successfully reunited with his birth mother and, later, his birth father.

Actually, his birth mother had wanted a reunion with him for years but believed the words she was told when she relinquished him: "You do not have the right to interfere in his life in the future." Jane was overjoyed when the searcher called her to tell her that her birth son wanted contact with her. For her, it was a dream come true.

For the first year after the reunion, all went well. Nick and Jane saw each other on a regular basis, and Nick was warmly welcomed by Jane's extended family (his extended birth family). After a few months of happy reunion activities, Nick realized his birth family had thirty-five years of history together that he knew nothing about. They were close because they had been a family during all the time Nick was growing up in his adoptive family. He said his birth family couldn't have been warmer or more inclusive, but he felt outside their family, different from all the other members. This brought up a new sadness in Nick and some anger as well—a new anger that his birth mother had placed him for adoption.

Nick said he felt he was being judged by his newly found birth family. He grew up in a small town and wasn't quite as sophisticated as his birth family. This made Nick uncomfortable when he was with them. He said that for the second time in his life, he found himself in a family where he felt he didn't fit.

Nick grew up in a loving family, although he says he felt like he was different, like he didn't fit in with his parents or other adopted siblings. He was hoping that a successful search would bring him some comfort and a sense of belonging to his birth family.

When this didn't happen to the extent that he wanted, he started to look inward at himself. Before his search, he just *felt* emotions. Now he was questioning *why* he felt like he did. He realized that during his adolescence and young adult life, he'd made some self-destructive choices in the people he associated with as well as in the activities he chose. Nick didn't feel like he had much self-esteem, particularly after being told by the adoption agency that his birth mother had not searched for him.

In the meetings, Nick's demeanor changed quite drastically as he went through various stages of his search. At first, when his search was thwarted, he was very quiet and sad. It was hard for him to express himself even in an understanding support group. His voice faltered, and he forced back tears.

After their reunion, Nick's birth mother attended some of the support group meetings. Nick had changed; he was jubilant and outgoing. He presented a drastic change from the dejected adoptee who first attended the meetings. After some time, Nick changed again; he became serious and introspective. He was now looking at his past thirty-five years through different, more knowledgeable eyes. He still felt many of the same emotions and had some of the same insecurities as before, but now he realized their source. He understands to some extent the whys of what he felt.

His relationship with his adoptive family has changed since his reunion. He is seeing them more because he doesn't want to hurt them by making them feel threatened by the time he spends with his new family. However, Nick says he wishes he had not been given up for adoption and had been raised by his birth mother. He feels that as hard as he has tried his whole life to fit into his adoptive family, it just isn't possible for him to feel that comfortable with them.

He likes his newly found extended birth family, but because of the time (thirty-five years) away from them, he feels like he will always be a stranger there too. If his birth mother had kept him, Nick feels he would belong in the right place and wouldn't be struggling with his doubts and self-esteem issues. No one can ever know, of course, but Nick feels he would have felt he was at home in his birth family, whereas he now entertains some anger toward his birth mother for not keeping him.

The successful reunion has had many good results. Nick says he feels more human, more alive. It appeared in these group sessions that Nick had been forced to think through many issues that have plagued him for years. He is perhaps more realistic as to the details of his life. His life is what it is. No one can go back to change it. The answer seems to lie in how Nick handles his life from now on. He has the choice to keep his adoption issues, which cause him frustration and unhappiness alive, or he can look at his life realistically. The missing piece of his personal puzzle has been found. He knows why he was placed for adoption, and he knows who he is.

He knows who he is according to the way he was raised, and he knows who he is according to the facts within his birth family. His job now is to meld these two images together to create the best person he can be. It appears to be hard for him to keep going without backsliding into self-pity and the feeling that no one understands him. Like all people, Nick has a lot to offer, but he has a lot of work ahead of him to bring all aspects of his life together. He needs to see his uniqueness and build on that.

Natalie Kimball, Adoptee

Natalie is a portrait of a forty-year-old adoptee who has a healthy, balanced perspective on adoption and all its potential issues. She is an adoptive parent's dream child, one who loved her parents dearly and couldn't imagine having any other parents.

She had a fairly uneventful childhood, but when she was sixteen years old, her parents suddenly divorced. Her mother discovered that her father was having an affair, and within a few months, their marriage was over. The second trauma in Natalie's life happened when she was thirty years old. After finding the whereabouts of her birth mother, she learned that her birth mother did not want to meet her.

Natalie is now happily married with four children. Her adoptive mother is deceased, and she has no contact with her adoptive father due to his controlling new wife. Natalie does have contact with a birth aunt and a birth cousin (daughter of the aunt). Both of these people are very reluctant to say anything about their family, so it is difficult for Natalie to learn about her birth family. It appears to be full of secrets or, at the very least, people who don't want to talk about their family.

In spite of this difficult situation, Natalie has a perspective that takes it all in stride. She says her adoptive mother was not a warm person, so the fact that her birth mother doesn't want contact with her is something she can accept. She knows about cold women. She doesn't like it, but she can accept it, hoping one day her birth mother will change her mind.

Although Natalie grew up with a cold mother, her father made Natalie feel loved and gave her a sense she truly was his beloved daughter. Natalie says she often felt that her mother was afraid that Natalie "would turn out to be like my birth mother [i.e., have a baby out of wedlock]." Natalie says that when she grew to be a young woman, she realized how her birth mother's unplanned pregnancy could happen.

Natalie has no judgment one way or the other about her birth mother but feels that her birth mother still feels the shame of her unplanned pregnancy. Her birth mother was able to hide her pregnancy by not gaining much weight, so she was able to keep her job all the way through the pregnancy. She took a few days off to have a baby and then returned to work.

"I think there was a lot of denial there," Natalie says. "She wasn't at a home for unwed mothers, where she could talk to other girls. She lived at home, worked, had her baby, and went back to work."

Even though Natalie does not have any interaction with her birth mother, she still says the search was a success in her mind. She doesn't take her mother's actions as a personal rejection. She looks upon it as her birth mother having a problem to deal with in not coming to terms with her unplanned pregnancy and subsequent placement of Natalie for adoption.

"The search made me feel complete," Natalie says. "It put actual living people in my life's beginning. The fact that they are real people makes me feel real. I don't feel like I dropped from the sky anymore. I know I have a real honest-to-goodness birth family. Sure, I'd like to get to know more about them, but for now, I'm happy just knowing they actually do exist." She goes on to say, "I don't want drama, bad drama, in my life right now. I don't want to force something that my birth mother doesn't want, may not be ready for. I do hope some day she will be ready, though."

Natalie is close to her sister, who is three years younger and also adopted. They've always been close. Natalie thinks many of her sister's life problems stem from her adoption issues. She says her sister isn't one bit interested in searching for her birth parents but asks Natalie about Natalie's progress with her birth family quite often. Natalie hopes her sister does search one day, saying that even though it doesn't end up like a Walt Disney movie, at least you validate your existence with real people who have real names.

In interviewing Natalie, one is impressed with the deep understanding she has of all the issues involved with all the people in her complicated, somewhat fragmented early years. She says she always felt her adoptive mother didn't accept her as quite good enough. Her mother was an indifferent person who, at times, made Natalie feel that she came from "bad stock," and she was afraid Natalie would turn out to be just like them. Fortunately, Natalie's adoptive father was her champion, but from the age of sixteen on after her parents divorced, Natalie was estranged from her father by his new wife, who felt that Natalie was a threat to the new marriage.

After finding out who her birth mother was and being rejected by her, Natalie again was made to feel outside the family. In spite of this, Natalie appears to be an understanding woman who says she can understand how people have problems, and those problems dictate some actions in their lives.

Some people could say that Natalie suffered two rather dramatic rejections in her life: first from her birth mother and later from her adoptive father. To Natalie's credit, she was able to see the circumstances surrounding both perceived rejections. In the first, she was born into circumstances where keeping your child was almost impossible. Natalie handled her second rejection by laying it at the feet of her father's new wife. Natalie did not take ownership of either rejection. Fortunately, she was mature and secure enough to do this.

Many adoptees feel rejected and take it personally. They hold on to this rejected feeling for years, even though intellectually they realize they were never known by their birth mothers so it cannot be a personal matter. Their birth mothers and their families made an adoption plan for a baby, not for the person the adoptee is.

One can see the difference in lives that have perspective and balance and those lives where adoptees hang on to their initial sense of rejection. The latter have not progressed to an understanding of being born into a society when young girls were not able to keep babies born outside of marriage. Taking their adoption placement personally can have a profound effect on their lives. They often find it hard to trust or have a lasting loving relationship because they suspect every subsequent person in their life may also reject them.

It is refreshing to interview a person who can step back from their own personal situation to analyze the situations that others are in and give them respect for their feelings and actions, even though they may not agree with them. Natalie is one of these people, and her life reflects the healthy way in which she views her circumstances within her adoptive family as well as within her birth family. She is her own woman and is making her own life. The words "generous spirit" come to mind when describing Natalie.

Lynn Thayer, Adoptee

Lynn – adoptee
Jim – her adopted brother

When Lynn was interviewed, she was in her midtwenties, a mother of two with her third child due in four months. Lynn has never been married, and all three of her children have different fathers.

"I was adopted into a wonderful, loving family, but I didn't turn out like all my friends did," Lynn said. "They did it right, and I got messed up in drugs and did it wrong. I really, really appreciate my parents now for sticking by me."

Lynn was adopted as an infant into a family with an adopted brother four years older. She said she and her brother were never close because of her brother's problems and the age difference of four years. Her brother, Jim, had many inherited issues, one being fetal alcohol syndrome. He had problems in school, and although his parents sought professional help for him throughout his childhood, nothing seemed to help. Jim got into trouble constantly, and because he had no conscience, his problems didn't bother him. He was in residential facilities much of his teenage years and eventually left his family and moved to another state.

Lynn was sexually abused by Jim when he was twelve and she was eight years old. Lynn was so young she didn't understand what was going on, so she didn't tell her parents for several months about this.

Lynn had been the happy, perfect daughter as a young child. She said she always felt positive about adoption because her parents talked positively about it. She said, "By contrast to what Jim was doing, I looked really good to my parents." In her midteens, Lynn entered the drug world, and her own world crashed after that. She dropped out of school, used drugs and alcohol, was gone from home for long periods of time, and engaged in the behavior that drugs and alcohol lead people into.

Lynn found herself in a correctional facility for a year's sentence after stealing a car when she was in her early twenties. She said it was then that she realized she was responsible for her behavior, and her parents couldn't help her this time. It was quite a revelation to her. After her release, Lynn said she wanted to make up for the time she was incarcerated, so she sought out drugs again. Her first pregnancy resulted from an all-night party.

This pregnancy, coupled with her recent incarceration, was a wake-up call for Lynn. She herself had problems caused by her birth mother's use of drugs, and Lynn vowed she would never do that to her own child. Lynn gave up drugs immediately and now says her children are her life. They keep her focused on a responsible way of life.

Lynn got her GED and works as a secretary in a business where she is well liked by her coworkers and does a good job of supporting her two children. She says she realizes she has problems with bad judgment when it comes to the men in her life. At the time of her interview, Lynn wondered aloud whether that was because of her learning disabilities, her manic depression, or her sexual abuse, or all combined. She plans to have her tubes tied after the delivery of her third child.

It was obvious during the interview that when Lynn said "My kids are my world," she truly meant it. She says she has no plans to marry because she wants to devote all her attention and efforts toward her children. Her feelings and efforts toward them are so concentrated that she doesn't want to dilute it with any other relationship.

Lynn is very close to her adoptive parents, says her mother now is her best friend, and says she has no desire to search for her birth parents. The fact that her birth mother used drugs right up until the day Lynn was delivered emphasizes for Lynn that she doesn't want to meet her. Lynn did say she would be interested in meeting her three older sisters, apparently kept by her birth mother. Lynn says she has some health and learning problems, obviously caused by her birth mother's drug use, and she might want more information about this in the future but for now says, "I really don't need that drama in my life that meeting my birth mother would cause."

Lynn says her adoptive mother tells her the reason she keeps having children is so she has someone who looks like her. Lynn agrees, and goes on to say, "I'd never give away my babies because I don't want them to feel the abandonment that I felt."

In her conversation, Lynn said that adoption was not much of an issue for her. She says her parents always talked about adoption and her birth parents in a positive way and said they would support any search for her birth parents. With the knowledge that Lynn has about her birth mother, Lynn feels she was given a second chance in life by being adopted and questions how she would have turned out if she had been kept by her birth mother.

The ongoing support Lynn was given by her adoptive parents was paramount to her straightening out her life. She says now that she is in her twenties; she can see things she didn't realize in her teens. She admires her parents greatly and says she can see things through her mother's eyes, which gives her a good perspective.

When asked if she felt she fit into her adoptive family, Lynn said, "I can't imagine myself being anywhere else. Yes, I do feel I fit and I belong. I didn't feel that way during my teen years, but now I see how much I'm like my mother. I find myself doing things just like she does. Their sticking with me through my drug use and incarceration is great motivation for me to live my life right. They've had enough unhappiness. I want to please them now. They are wonderful people."

Standing by their children through thick and thin, these adoptive parents are an example of how their efforts can provide a happy conclusion, at least a partial happy conclusion. Lynn's parents, who are profiled under adoptive parents later in the book, went through very difficult years when Lynn and her brother were in their teens. Their adoptive mother, who is an administrator in a large business, said these years were a challenge. During work breaks, when others were relating events about their families, she often went out into the hall where she could cry freely. It broke her heart that she didn't share those same parenting joys. Jim did eventually end up in prison, but Lynn and her children now bring satisfaction and joy into their lives.

Wendy Morgan, Adoptee

Wendy – adoptee
Wanda – twin sister, adopted together

Wendy said she had the best adoptive parents she could imagine. She and her twin sister were the only children raised by two wonderful parents. Wendy said she and her twin look different and are different. She was more of a tomboy while her sister was more feminine. She wishes they were more similar.

In her forties, Wendy wanted to search for their birth mother. After being found by a professional searcher, their birth mother rejected Wendy and her twin sister, Wanda, saying she didn't want contact with them. This rejection was a blow to both of the women, particularly to Wanda, who really didn't want to search in the first place because she dreaded the fact they might be rejected again. Wendy had convinced her to search, and their adoptive parents were supportive of the search.

Wendy said she had always fantasized about her birth mother in a positive way. Once she knew some facts about their birth mother, particularly that she was only eighteen when she gave birth, the fantasy was gone. Wendy felt some empathy for their birth mother while Wanda did not.

After the rejection and knowledge that she would never see her birth mother, Wendy asked a friend, who was a private investigator, to search for more information. He was able to find their birth mother's name and a high school picture, and Wendy says that gave her the closure she was looking for. She felt a great sense of relief that she had that piece of her puzzle. She went on to say that if their birth mother ever changed her mind and said she would reunite with the twins, she would in a heartbeat but Wanda would not.

In the interview, when asked if Wendy would rather have been raised by her birth mother or her adoptive parents, she put her head back, looked up at the ceiling, and said, "Oh, God. I hate that question. I've been thinking about it." After thinking out loud, expounding all the pros and cons of both situations, Wendy announced that she couldn't answer the question, couldn't make the choice because she still feels a genetic pull to her birth family. She says she often scans the obituaries looking for her birth mother's name.

The surprise of all this was that she couldn't decide. Most interviewees—even those who said their adoptive families weren't the best, in their opinion—answered that same question with "I would definitely want to be raised by my adoptive family because they provided more of a healthy environment."

After Wendy's rejections and saying throughout the interview that her parents were wonderful and provided love and support, she found it hard to answer the question. Does this show how very deep the biological bond is and how much Wendy misses it? Perhaps so. Her dilemma was the choice between the self-expressed wonderful life she had with adoptive parents compared with an unknown life with the birth mother who did not keep the twins at birth and rejected a connection with them forty years later. Logic would say there isn't much of a choice here until you take into account the power of the genetic bond – and Wendy's lack of actually experiencing it.

Ed Johnston, Adoptee

Ed – adoptee
Aunt Sarah – sister of Ed's birth mother

Ed was forty-five years old when he made contact with his aunt Sarah, the sister of his birth mother. He'd always known that he would eventually search for his birth family. He felt guilty about searching, so his adoptive parents never knew.

After the phone call to his aunt Sarah and her questions—"Where have you been?" followed by "How soon can you get here?"—Ed started out on a four-hour drive. He passed through the town where his daughter was in college. He called ahead and said he wanted to switch cars with his daughter, who had a red convertible. Ed left her the conservative family car and proceeded on to meet his aunt and some other relatives in a "sharp car."

"I wanted them to see how cool I was," Ed said. "I wanted them to see what they'd missed all these years. I wasn't about to show up in a family SUV."

Ed shed tears a few times during our interview. One of the episodes was when he told of the comment his aunt Sarah made to him during their reunion: "If I'd still been at home when you were born, you never would have been given up for adoption. We don't give away our own."

"I could have been someone 180 degrees dif—" and then the tears stopped him from finishing his sentence.

The reunion with his aunt was positive, but other members of his birth family didn't want to meet him. Aunt Sarah told Ed that his birth father drove his birth mother to two different cities to get an abortion, but no one would perform it, so Ed was born.

Ed is very bright but as a child did live with some undiagnosed learning disabilities. His aunt told him his grandfather owned an accounting firm, which encouraged Ed to do more with his life. In his forties, he went back to school and got a master's in finance. He said he rarely took notes but could remember everything.

Ed did not have a good relationship with either his adoptive mother or father. In his teens, this became such an issue for him that he stopped calling them Mom and Dad and started calling them by their given names. Ed said he felt his adoptive parents really didn't parent at all. This only exaggerated his feeling of being abandoned, not just by one set of parents but by two.

Ed's younger brother was also adopted, but the two didn't get along very well. His brother was a tough kid and a bully. The two didn't have contact for years, but his brother called one day to say he was terminally ill and all alone. He moved in with Ed and his wife and lived with them until he died eight months later.

Throughout the interview, Ed showed a glimmer of the wise-guy attitude in him in a charming, humorous way. At one point, he stated, "Don't discount my pain because of my humor. I'm a pro at covering up." He said he'd always felt guilty about wanting to search until a priest one day said to him, "You're the young man searching for his roots." This helped him by putting a new perspective on his desire to search.

Ed was sad when he related that he had an uncle who had two daughters and no sons. One day, when Ed was a young boy, his uncle bemoaned the fact that he didn't have a son to do things with. Ed asked why his uncle didn't take him to a ball game. His uncle's answer was "Because you're adopted."

Ed remembers being in his crib, waking up from a nap. He had a dirty diaper, and remembers his mother saying "You are a dirty, nasty child." At age sixty-five, telling this story brought tears to his eyes.

He also remembers being called stupid because he had trouble in school, undoubtedly related to his undiagnosed dyslexia. In spite of the fact that he was a pilot in the Korean War, a successful businessman, and had earned a master's in finance, Ed became quietly sad when he remembered the label he was called as a child. To this day, he is sensitive to the word *stupid*.

Ed was one of the very few who when asked who would he rather have been raised by answered, "My birth family, no question about it."

Ed said he doesn't like funerals and rarely goes. He did go to his aunt Sarah's (whom he had contact with for twelve years before she died). Ed choked up and couldn't talk for a minute when he said he was very moved upon finding his birth mother's grave site.

"I imagine she became very real to you at that moment," one of the interviewers offered.

Ed nodded and quietly said, "Yeah."

This interview showed us a man who grew up with loss and rejection. His childhood was not conducive to helping him become a successful adult, but the man we interviewed was. The tears he shed while talking were tears of pain that for him will probably never go away. He's developed for himself a life of success and accomplishment in spite of the feeling in his younger years that he was all alone. It's interesting that after he made contact with his birth family in his midforties, he went back to school to get an advanced degree –a degree in the same field as his birth grandfather.

Beth Lawson, Adoptee

Beth – adoptee
Midge – her half birth sister
Jan –her birth mother

Beth is a thirty-six-year-old adoptee. She is like many others in that she always felt different from her adoptive family members and didn't feel understood but also stated that she is glad her adoptive family raised her instead of her birth mother, whom she met four years ago. What sets Beth apart from the other adoptees we interviewed is that she has spent years in therapy because of her diagnosed depression, and is very much aware of and in touch with her feelings. She can answer every question directly and honestly because she has thought about her life more than most have.

Beth lives in the same city as both her adoptive parents and her birth parents. She has an ongoing relationship with Jan, her birth mother, but her attempts to meet her birth father have been met with silence on his part. Beth saw him one morning in the parking lot of the company he owns. She had done some detective work and had a picture of him. Beth stated that the minute she laid eyes on him, she knew who he was. She stayed in her car, and as much as she wanted to approach him, she held herself back, knowing that it would be an unfair shock for him. The only time during the interview when she had tears in her eyes was when she was talking about her birth father. She said the thought of him not answering her letters cuts her deeply as a hurtful rejection. Beth has had years of therapy, but she still feels the pain very deeply. Her birth mother was sixteen and her birth father was seventeen when Beth was born. Her birth father ended his relationship with Beth's birth mother upon hearing of her pregnancy.

Beth is close to her sister who is three years older than she, also adopted. They consider each other as best friends and have a mutual understanding of what they perceive to be their parents' less-than-perfect attitude toward parenting. It involves more criticism than praise. They are "good" daughters and see their parents regularly but have a hard time with the ongoing negative attitude they observe.

Adoption was not spoken of in their household while they were growing up, and the few times Beth asked questions about her birth family, she was given short answers and the impression that this was not a subject to be brought up again. Beth did an official adoption search when she was thirty and found her birth mother, as well as a half-sister, at that time.

Beth's life was in a much-higher socioeconomic strata than her birth mother's and half-sister's. Beth says her adoptive parents indulged both her and her adopted sister with many material advantages. They went to private schools and private colleges. Her birth sister lived a life with fewer material advantages and fewer educational opportunities. There are some ongoing issues with

Midge, Beth's birth half-sister, surrounding this discrepancy of life's opportunities. Beth is single, independent, and owns her own company while Midge is married with young children. They find little ground for commonality. Their lifestyles, both in childhood and the present, are very different from one another, although Beth does see some similarities in their personalities.

Beth's ongoing relationship with her birth mother, Jan, is good although she looks upon her as a friend, and not a mother figure. Beth is very strong and independent and has a strong work ethic, holding down several jobs at the same time. Her birth family is more relaxed and not nearly as active and focused as Beth. All along, Beth says she fantasized that her birth mother would be a wealthy, world traveling business woman (what Beth always wanted to be growing up) and it wasn't until a week before the reunion when she read a letter from her birth mother that her fantasy dissolved. She was disappointed that the reality did not match her long held view.

Beth says she is glad she has met her birth mother because it has filled the void and emptiness inside of her, but there are times when the relationship may be a bit tense or awkward, and she is ambivalent about the fact that she opened Pandora's box. At times, she wonders if it was the right thing to do. She now has more family relationships to deal with in her everyday life.

Beth says her relationship with her adoptive mother is better since the reunion, but her relationship with her father has more tension. He and her adoptive mother don't want to know about Beth's birth family or her activities with them. If they find out some past or proposed meeting of Beth and her birth mother, each parent will say, "Now don't tell your mother (or father)." Beth feels this is putting her in the middle of an awkward situation. They may be trying to protect each other from perceived hurt that Beth has a relationship with her birth family, but Beth feels this is her parents' issue, not hers. Still, she can't help feeling responsible for their uneasiness.

It is interesting to see the conflict in the two identities Beth is dealing with. She says she is very much like her birth mother in being somewhat of a type A personality with liberal, open minded moral and political views, but still she was raised in an advantaged manner which ties her to her adoptive family even though her personal views differ from theirs. She feels both a common bond, as well as distancing factors, with both her adoptive and birth families. She can't slide easily and comfortably into either one. She is continuing to develop herself into being a strong, self sufficient, well balanced person. One can sense her need to be independent, and she works hard to defend her own personal boundaries so that she can deal with both families – both of which give her happiness, as well as challenges.

Chris Schmidt, Adoptee

Chris—adoptee
George – her birth father

Chris is any adoptive parent's dream child. She was raised as an only child, loved her parents dearly, and couldn't imagine having any other parents. She was particularly close to her mother, who always told her that she always dreamed of having a daughter. Chris's mother had a wonderful relationship with her own mother, and was looking forward to that same kind of relationship with her daughter. Chris fulfilled that dream.

Chris always felt close to her parents and didn't look at adoption as any big deal. She was made to feel she was a gift in her parents' lives. As Chris said, "There are so many large looming events in one's life, like getting a job, marriage, having children. I never thought of adoption as one of those life-changing events. I just knew I was loved and cherished and couldn't imagine not being who I was."

When Chris was in her late twenties, she approached her adoption agency for non-identifying information and was told that her birth father had put a request in her file that he would like to meet her. This isn't what Chris was looking for at the time, but after thinking about it for a while, she said she would like to meet him. Actually, Chris said that she rarely thought about her birth father. She was always concerned about her birth mother and hoped she didn't have too hard a time with her unplanned pregnancy. Chris was concerned that her mother might be shunned by family and friends as a result of this and felt badly that this might be the scenario.

Chris lives in the Midwest, and both her birth parents live on the East Coast (where Chris was born). Her birth parents never married but remained in touch with each other on a friendly basis over the years. Chris flew to New York and was met by both of them at the airport. She then spent three days with her birth father in Manhattan and then went to New Jersey to spend three days with her birth mother. Chris said, "As you can imagine, it was an intense week!"

That reunion took place eight years ago. Although Chris was born and raised on the East Coast, by choice she now lives in the Midwest. She was raised in a professional family with conservative values, and meeting her birth parents was quite a shock for her. Chris was born in the late sixties and says her birth parents still embrace the open hippie lifestyle. She finds their values are very different from what she is comfortable with, and says, "Thank goodness they didn't raise me. Who knows what I would have become."

Chris is a physician, happily married with two children. She says she can envision who she might be if she would have stayed with her birth parents. Her birth mother tells Chris that she never wanted to be a mother because she knew she wouldn't be good at it. Chris looks upon her birth mother as a nice friend but surely not a mother figure. On the other hand, Chris's birth father, George, never wanted to relinquish Chris and has been longing for contact with his daughter ever since her birth.

Now that the reunion has taken place, psychology experts would say her birth father has a hard time with proper personal boundaries.

Although he lives hundreds of miles away from Chris, he visits at least once each year for a week. Chris is uncomfortable with him and discourages him from visiting, but he won't take no for an answer. In an e-mail, he asked if July or August would be a good time for a visit. Chris e-mailed back that neither month would be good. He then e-mailed back several dates in July that he could come. Chris responded again that none of the dates would work out. George e-mailed back that he had made an airline reservation for July 15.

Chris keeps saying he is a nice man, a good man, but she just doesn't like him intruding in her life. At first, George stayed with Chris and her husband, but recently, he has stayed at a hotel in town. His longing for his daughter seems to transcend logic in that he acknowledges that he needs Chris more than she needs him, and still he insists on visiting even when he knows he is not welcomed.

To Chris, her adoption was never much of an issue in her life. It was not something she thought about very much. She was a happy daughter of loving parents. She now has birth parents who are also a part of her life. Chris says she enjoys her birth mother (who never wanted to be a mother) because she is not intrusive. They contact each other warmly from time to time, and it is a pleasant woman-to-woman exchange. Her relationship with her birth father is very different as their needs for each other don't mesh. George wants a good frequent relationship with his daughter, but Chris says she has a father and doesn't need a second one.

Throughout the interview, Chris was reluctant to say anything bad about George, but when asked if she was sorry she went ahead with the reunion, Chris thought through her words very carefully. "If I knew they were happy and my birth didn't mess up their lives, then that's all I would need to know," she answered. "I don't need to have a relationship with either of them as I have a family already. I don't look upon them as family, just as nice people. Unfortunately, my birth father doesn't see it this way. He looks upon me as family, and I'm not. One time, someone referred to him as my father, and I cringed. He is not my father. I have a father and love him dearly. To have the word *father* applied to my birth father was offensive to me. I never belonged anywhere but in my family, where I am today. I am a product of their love and would never want to be anywhere else. After meeting my birth parents, I appreciate my life even more. I shudder to think of who I might be if I had not been adopted by my parents."

Fred Sutton, Adoptee

Fred was an interview subject who didn't have any controversy to report. He said adoption didn't appear to have much, if any, effect on his life. He was in his early fifties at the time we interviewed him, and his life appeared to be very normal, happy, and under control.

Fred's birth mother kept him during the first few months of his life even though she could not provide a steady home for him. She deposited him with various relatives, asking them to care for her baby. At some point, when Fred was a few months old, he came to the attention of authorities and a doctor and was taken away from his family due to his malnutrition state. A few months after that, he was adopted as the first of his family's two adopted sons.

Fred said he always felt loved, wanted, and special. Adoption was not discussed in the family, leading Fred to believe it was not a big deal. He said he was sure his younger brother felt the same way about being adopted. Fred stated that his life would have been the same if he had been a biological son to his parents. He was treated like all the other children he grew up with and didn't feel any negative effects because he was an adopted child. He felt he had the same status as his friends who were biological children.

Fred's adoptive mother was still alive at the time of our interview, and Fred mentioned that she, at age ninety-two, had just given him some adoption papers, saying, "You might be interested in this." Fred said he remembered asking his parents when he was a young boy if they knew anything about his birth parents, and they said they did not. Fred took this at face value, and it became a closed subject. Fred was surprised to be given these papers now and more surprised to see that his birth mother had given him a name. He said he showed the paper to his brother and said, "Look at this. I was a real person, name and all."

The papers had the name of his birth mother, her age, and the name she had given him, as well as the name of the hospital where he was born. Fred said this was the first time in his life he actually felt a little curiosity about his roots.

This interview was lacking in drama and heavy in normalcy. Upon leaving, Fred said the questions we asked of him did pique his interest in searching for his birth mother or her family.

A week or so after the interview, Fred called and said he had been doing more thinking and he would like to try to search. His birth mother's name was very ethnic and very unusual, both her first and last name. I thought just a simple Internet effort might find the answer for him.

It did. Since Fred's birth certificate gave the age of Fred's mother at the time of his birth, we knew she would be eighty-three now. We entered her name, and a listing came up for an eighty-three-year-old woman who lived in Ohio. I called the number and asked for the name on Fred's birth certificate. I was told she wasn't there, so I continued by saying why I was calling, that I knew a man who was searching for his birth mother. The woman said the name was her sister's name, but she had died fifteen years earlier. We talked a bit more. She appeared very friendly but didn't ask at all about Fred. She said her sister had never married and never had a baby.

After I hung up, I told Fred that I'm sure we had found the right person. It's possible she could have died fifteen years earlier, it's possible she never had a baby, it's possible she could have had a baby but no family members knew, and it's also possible that the woman whom I spoke with was Fred's mother. We will never know.

Fred appeared to take this as a final answer and didn't show any emotion. He had wonderful parents and a wonderful life, and he said adoption had a minimal effect on his life. Either all this was true, or he was a very good actor. He died a year later.

SECTION III

9

Birth Parents

Birth parents in general had a wide range of opinions. Most of these birth parents gave birth at a time when it was socially unacceptable to raise a child who was born out of wedlock. Most birth parents were teenagers at the time, and their parents took over, making plans for the adoption. Some birth parents, in looking back now as adults, were very angry that they had no power at the time to keep their baby while others, analyzing their lives, were grateful their baby was raised and loved by a couple who could give their child stability and advantages the birth parent could not.

Below is an example of some of the questions asked of birth parents who were now in their forties, fifties, or sixties and could look back from that perspective:

- How old were you when your child was born?
- Were you married or single?
- What was the relationship between you and the other birth parent? Was it a long- or short-term relationship?
- Had the two of you talked of marriage either before the pregnancy or after the pregnancy?

- If you were the birth father, did you have concerns that this may not be your child?
- As a birth father, did you know of the pregnancy at the time? Did you have any say in the future of the baby? Were you able to emotionally support each other, or were you separated by your parents?
- How did the parents of your boyfriend/girlfriend treat you? Were you the one they blamed for the unplanned pregnancy?
- What was the reaction of your family when you told them of the pregnancy? Did they support you? Was the birth mother whisked out of town to give birth so no one would know?
- How did your family and those who knew make you feel? Were you made to feel guilty and that you were a bad person? Has this feeling lingered over the years?
- Did you feel you had any power in the decision making as to what would happen to your baby?
- Did you see your baby after its birth? Did you hold your baby?
- How often did you think about your baby throughout the years? How did this affect your holidays and special occasions?
- Did you stay in contact with the other birth parent?
- Did you ever think about a reunion with your birth child? Did you feel you had the right to contact him/her? Did you want them to contact you instead? Did you worry about how they would look upon you?
- If you've had a reunion, how has this changed your view on life, your view of yourself?
- If you've reunited, how does your current family (husband or wife and other children) react to this?
- If reunited, do you see yourself as strangers or was there an instant connection?
- Hindsight—Did the adoptive family raise your/their child in a way you would have if you'd been in a position to do so?

- Was adoption the best decision for your child?
- How has being a birth parent changed the direction of your decisions and your life?

We found there to be quite a contrast in attitude concerning not being able to raise a child you had given birth to. Some birth mothers were still very angry after forty or fifty years that their child was taken from them, and they were powerless at the time to stop this. Their anger was vented toward society and the adoptive parents who raised "their" child. Others, looking back at the times, were very grateful that their child had a healthy, happy, loving home with two parents. They admitted that at their young age they could not have provided this. Many said their birth child would have been shunted around from relative to relative while they tried to finish their education so they could support their child.

10

Birth-Parent Profiles

Robin Harper, Birth Mother

Robin — birth mother
Sandy – her birth son

Robin has cried many tears. She had a relatively normal childhood, but her life changed drastically when she was impregnated by her high school boyfriend. They'd dated for a year and in their senior year became sexually active, which resulted in her pregnancy. Her boyfriend insisted the baby wasn't his, which was devastating for Robin.

Robin sat through our three-hour interview presenting herself for most of that time as a well-adjusted, well-controlled individual who had come to terms with her life and was doing well. She had a quiet, dulcet voice, which matched her sweet demeanor. Toward the end of the interview, however, she became emotional and shed tears as she talked about being rejected by her baby's father and having to give up her son into the unknown world of adoption.

In 1959, Robin was nineteen years old, and giving up her son was just the first of many losses she experienced. She suffered severe depression and had psychiatric counseling and shock treatments after that event. She said she felt very alone after the birth of her son and had no support from anyone.

Her first loss was the loss of her birth son, but in addition, she lost the birth father whom she loved but who would not marry her. Robin wanted to marry, but he did not.

Shortly thereafter, her mother died and her father remarried within six months. Her father's new wife would not allow Robin into their home. Her brother married and moved away, and three years after that, Robin's father died. Robin was still in her twenties and very alone.

Upon hearing of her pregnancy, Robin's parents were rather matter-of-fact, very practical, with not much emotion being shown. When she was three months pregnant, she was sent to a town two hours away to live in a wage home. The family where she was placed had a three-year-old adopted daughter, and it was Robin's job to care for the little girl while the girl's mother (also pregnant) continued to work.

After the birth of her son, Robin said she never felt whole—until she was reunited with him forty years later. She said that for years, she thought of her son multiple times throughout the day and prayed for him every night.

In her twenties, Robin was diagnosed with depression and suffered from this for seven years. In addition to all her personal losses within her family, at age twenty-three, she married a man who was moved every year or two by the company he worked for. Robin didn't have time to steady herself.

In discussing aspects of her life, Robin stated that she was not angry at the birth father but still felt much anger toward the system in those days, which put so much pressure on unwed mothers that they felt they had no choice but to give up their babies. She blamed the social workers, the lawyers, and all who were involved in her situation. She was treated humanely but not sympathetically.

She was not allowed to see her baby; however, she snuck down one evening to the hospital nursery to look at him. Robin said her baby's eyes were open, and he looked at her. One of her lowest moments was a few days after her son was born and her milk came in. She cried and cried, thinking of her hungry baby now among strangers.

When asked if coping with her loss became easier with time, she said, "You don't forget, you don't forget at all. You're always looking for the child you gave away. Mother's Day was the hardest."

Robin married a few years after her first son's birth and had two more children. She said it was always hard when she was asked how many children she had because she always answered two, knowing she really had three. She says she is still secretive about her first pregnancy. She doesn't tell anyone.

It took many years of searching before Robin found her first son, Sandy. Sandy said he'd never thought of searching for her. After Robin found his address in Texas, she wrote him a sixteen-page letter, which he never answered. A year later, he had a serious car accident and lost his job. Shortly after that, he did write back to Robin. He was living several states away, and once they had made contact, there was communication by letter for the first two years. That eventually moved into e-mail and a few phone calls now and then. Robin is angry at Sandy's adoptive parents, who are uncomfortable with Sandy having a relationship with Robin. One time, Sandy had planned a trip to her state to meet her and then cancelled it because his adoptive parents were upset about it.

A couple of years after that, Robin and her husband were in Texas on business, and Robin asked Sandy if he would meet with her. He didn't tell his adoptive parents, but he said he would meet. They had several days together, catching up on forty years of being apart. Robin said it was wonderful.

When asked what changed after their reunion, Robin said that she no longer carries the guilt she's carried for forty years. She now feels whole and as good as anyone else. The part of her life that was taken away is now back. She stated strongly that after giving up Sandy, she vowed to never again allow anyone else to make a decision for her. She's stuck to this her whole life.

In our interview, Robin said she was grateful to Sandy's adoptive parents for raising him, but it was obvious she had strong feelings about them. She told us she could have done just as good a job of raising Sandy as they did. She said it was hard to refer to them as 'your mom' and 'your dad.' She learned Sandy had to pay his own way through college while Robin and her husband paid tuition and expenses for their two children. Robin felt guilty about this and was resentful toward Sandy's parents because she knew they had enough money to pay his way.

Robin and Sandy have only met once for a few days in Texas. They contact each other a couple times a month but have no immediate plans to meet again. Robin thinks the adoptive parents are an influence in this. She's asked Sandy to visit her and meet his two half-siblings, but he doesn't come.

There has been an ongoing sadness in Robin's life because of her high school pregnancy. Throughout the interview, she never mentioned the names of her husband or two subsequent children. Her first pregnancy (and loss) appeared to direct her life. It pervaded her marriage, her parenting of her two subsequent children, and her overall look on life. She says she can offer things to Sandy that his adoptive parents can't offer him, like blood relatives, family stories and pictures, and people who look like him. Robin says Sandy has her eye and hair color, her ears, and her long fingers and toes. Her demeanor is one of sadness when she talks about him. She has him in her life, but still, she doesn't. When she looks at him, she says, "I know he's mine. Yep, he's mine."

But is he really? What would Sandy say?

Rita Randall, Birth Mother and Adoptee

Rita – birth mother
Harry — her birth son

Rita Randall, age seventy-nine at the time of our interview, was one of our first interviewees. After hearing her story, I wondered how she was able to come through her life as a sane person. She experienced so much trauma that being a birth mother, as well as an adoptee, were just facts in her life, along with many others. Both these situations, however, had profound effects on her, and many of her problems were caused by these two situations. Not only did she appear to still be sane after all she went through, but she was a charming and compassionate lady as well.

Rita was born to a married couple and lived with them until the age of two, at which time her maternal grandfather's new domineering wife wrested her away from her biological parents after seeing Rita wrapped in a blanket and sleeping in an orange crate. The whole family was afraid of this controlling woman. Rita's father tried to get his daughter back one day and sped away with Rita in the car while the step-grandmother was holding on to the car. The step-grandmother did get Rita back but blamed Rita constantly for the injuries she had sustained while trying to hold on to the moving car. Rita's parents were terrified of Rita's step-grandmother, who forbade them to have any contact with Rita. Eventually they melted away from her life completely.

Rita's childhood was a nightmare at the hands of this step-grandmother who formally adopted her. Rita called her an evil woman, and to escape, Rita married at age eighteen. Her husband didn't want children, but Rita got pregnant right away and bore a daughter. Shortly after, her husband volunteered for the army and asked a friend of his to look out for Rita while he was in the service. This friend raped Rita, and she bore a son from this rape. Rita wanted to keep her baby, but the step-grandmother interfered, forcing Rita to give the baby up for adoption. Rita said her hatred of her step-grandmother was so strong that it clouded her feeling of grief for her lost son.

Rita divorced her physically abusive husband when he returned from the army, and she soon after married an older man to give herself and her young daughter some stability away from the interfering step-grandmother. Three more children resulted from this union, but this was a bad marriage, and Rita divorced him while she was in her midthirties. An important factor in this divorce was that her husband's mother lived with them but was outwardly opposed to their marriage and sabotaged it in many ways. She was a petty woman and wanted to make Rita look inept. For instance, she would turn up the heat under a dish Rita was cooking on the stove and then, when it burned, would point out that Rita couldn't even cook right.

At this juncture in her life, Rita decided to live alone with her four children. This proved to be more successful, and to this day, all of them are very close. In an ironic twist, Rita was the only relative available when her step-grandmother became terminally ill with cancer, so Rita, with four young children at home, went to her grandmother's house three times a day to feed her and change her clothes, bedding, etc.

Rita told no one of her rape and of being forced to relinquish her baby son. She kept this from her second husband and other children. She felt a loss and void in her life but didn't want others to feel the same. No one knew. In later years, Rita tried to search for the son she had given up for adoption, but she was not successful.

When Rita was in her sixties, Harry, the son whom she had relinquished, found her. Both his adoptive parents had died, and Harry, who was the executor of their estates, discovered that his father had donated money monthly to an adoption agency. It was through them that he found his birth mother, Rita.

Now, Rita tells everyone her story. The first part of her life was very bad, but her children, now all five of them, give her much satisfaction and joy. The son she relinquished lives in another state, but he calls her every Wednesday at 7:30 a.m. As she says, "We never run out of conversation."

It was interesting to hear Rita tell her story with relative objectivity. She said she hated, absolutely hated her stepgrandmother who stole her away from her parents and then took her second child away, but after so many years, she was tired of carrying around her anger. She had a lot of emotional debris to go through, but in order to survive, she felt she had to forgive this woman who affected her life so adversely.

One cannot help but admire the woman Rita has become. During our interview, she spoke without anger or resentment, just factually. With so many toxic people in her young life, it is a tribute to Rita and others like her who overcome adversity and pain. She said she swore to herself as a girl that she would never grow up to be like her stepgrandmother. To her credit, and with great effort not to let bitterness or resentment form who she became, she followed through with this promise to herself. She was successful. She was an inspiration to us as interviewers.

Chad Jackson, Birth Father

Chad – birth father
Lucy – birth mother
Earl – their birth son

Chad's story is an almost perfect example of how a reunion can drastically change lives. When interviewing Chad, it was obvious that even though he is mild mannered, he is euphoric that he found his birth son when his son was forty-one years old.

Chad and Lucy dated in their last year of high school, and Lucy gave birth to Earl when she was seventeen. Chad was nineteen at the time. Chad wanted to marry Lucy and keep their baby, but both sets of parents were against this. Neither family was harshly judgmental or hard on Chad and Lucy, but it was obvious in 1962 that with their not being married, their unplanned pregnancy would lead to adoption. When Chad heard that Lucy had gone to the hospital to give birth, he went immediately there to see her but was told he (as the boyfriend) could see neither her nor his baby. His son was five days old when he finally saw him the one and only time, until forty-one years later. Lucy was devastated she had to give up her son.

Chad and Lucy went on with their lives, staying in touch with each other, and decided to marry two years later. Chad now says he never would have married Lucy if they had not had a birth son. He felt the responsibility to take care of her. They had two more sons after their marriage. Their marriage was built around the bond they had having given birth to a son and then having to relinquish him. The marriage was built on guilt and remorse and ended after ten years.

Chad never married again while Lucy went on to have multiple marriages. Chad said the relinquishment of their first son was very much an issue in both their lives. They were both searching for a part of their lives that was missing and felt that loss on an ongoing basis.

Chad searched for some time, hoping to find Earl, who, at the same time, was also searching for his birth parents. While Earl was in his late thirties, Chad found out his name and location, but when he called his son, the voice on the other end of the phone said Earl wasn't there.

During this period, Chad was cutting his lawn one day and noticed a car parked across the street with a man in it watching him. He stayed parked for an hour, but whenever Chad would look at him, the man would look away. Chad knew it was his birth son. Another time, before meeting each other, Earl followed Chad to a restaurant and sat at a table nearby without making any contact.

After one of the many calls to Earl (who said Earl wasn't there), Chad's phone rang fifteen minutes later, and the voice said he was Earl. It took a couple more years before they met face-to-face.

At the time of our interview, Chad said his three sons are very close. In fact, his sons go on fishing trips together. Earl has never married, but Chad's two subsequent sons are married with children.

Chad said the first question he asked Earl was if he had had a good childhood. Chad was greatly relieved when Earl said he had wonderful parents and two siblings.

Chad said losing his first son haunted him his whole life. The fact that Earl has two full brothers may have played a role in this thinking. All three of his children have the same mother and father, but his first child had been lost. When asked if he felt close to Earl, Chad said that in a way he felt closer to Earl than to the two subsequent sons because Earl had not been in his life as long. He says their finding each other was a miracle.

It's interesting to play the what-if game in a situation like this. How much of an influence was Earl's relinquishment on both Chad and Lucy personally, as well as how integral was it in their failed marriage? If all three sons had not been full siblings, would Chad have worked so hard to find his first "lost" son? The euphoria and joy he obviously feels now would not be present if he and Lucy had raised their three children under normal circumstances. The contrast from guilt and remorse to reunion and completion is a dramatically large gap. Chad's subsequent sons lived with Lucy after their divorce but asked to live with Chad as they got older. One son told Chad he wished Chad had come for them both years earlier because their mother was so busy dating, marrying, and divorcing.

When Chad was asked if he thought his birth son, Earl, was better off raised by his adoptive family rather than by Chad and Lucy, Chad's response was that Earl was raised by a loving family and, with no question, was better off there. His other two sons were raised in a dysfunctional divorced family. Quite a dilemma—wishing his first son was actively a part of their family all through the years, only to come to the realization that he was better off not being raised there after all.

Chad said Earl is a very well-balanced individual living a successful, comfortable life. Earl owns two hundred acres outside a small town and raises cattle in addition to working in the construction business of his adoptive father. Chad mentioned several times that at age forty-one, Earl is in a much better place in life than he, Chad, had been at that same age. Chad is euphoric now that his three sons are all acquainted with each other and enjoying each other. It took them a while to get there, taking different routes, but Chad is thoroughly enjoying the happy, satisfying results.

Betty Lerner, Birth Mother

Betty – birth mother
Emma – her birth daughter

Betty is an example of the strong ongoing effect her unplanned pregnancy had throughout her life.

In our interview, Betty stated that she was an insecure teenager who desperately needed a relationship. She stated that she thought getting pregnant would cement her relationship with her high school boyfriend of two years. It did not. Their daughter was born when Betty was seventeen years old. The birth father took no responsibility for the situation and left Betty in shock and disappointment to handle her pregnancy by herself. He left town soon afterward to join the air force, and Betty thinks his parents never knew of the pregnancy.

During high school, the two had talked of marriage sometime in the future. Now that she was alone with her pregnancy, she said she felt her condition was like a piece of dirty laundry she had to get rid of.

Betty wasn't particularly close to her parents, and they were extremely ashamed and mortified when they learned about their daughter's pregnancy. It wasn't talked about much other than to make plans about what to do about it. Betty was three months pregnant when she graduated from high school and was immediately sent out of town to a home for unwed mothers. Betty said the nuns were kind to her, and her pregnancy was not too bad.

However, the birth of her baby and the process of relinquishing her daughter were traumatic.

Throughout our interview, Betty was soft-spoken and sweet. She spoke slowly and deliberately and chose her words carefully. When asked about the birth of her daughter and the time afterward, tears accompanied her words. Betty was allowed to see her baby just once but was not allowed to touch her or hold her. As more tears flowed, Betty said those were dark days.

Her parents weren't ready to have her return home immediately, so she went to stay with friends for a short time. Upon returning home, her pregnancy and her baby were never discussed.

While in high school, Betty had planned to go to college, but a short time after giving birth and returning home, she found a job at a local company instead. The birth father was off in the air force, and her parents were distant, and Betty felt very alone. For a short time, she dated a man the age of her father because she felt safe with him. She never thought of it as long-term, although he did. After a year of working, she realized she needed to change her life, so while still living at home, she decided to save enough money to go to college. Her parents didn't support this idea either financially or philosophically. She was on her own.

The thought of a large university terrified Betty, so she applied to a small Catholic school about a hundred miles from her home. When she had enough money for one year, she enrolled. Fortunately, with summer employment and employment on the campus, Betty was able to graduate in four years.

Betty found employment after graduation but went through years of therapy for depression. She didn't think the pregnancy alone caused her depression, but it was a factor. Almost from the beginning, she put a letter to her daughter in her file at Catholic Charities, hoping her daughter would one day want to find her.

Betty waited for thirty more years before marrying at age forty-seven. She wrestled with depression and trust and intimacy issues all that time. Betty said that in the era in which she gave birth, the young mothers were told to be secretive so that society would not know of their shameful act. She said it was the repression of all her emotions, not just grieving for her lost daughter, that contributed greatly to her ongoing depression. It took years of work with a therapist to unlock her feelings and deal with them.

When her birth daughter, Emma, was forty-two years old (and Betty was fifty-nine), Emma did contact Catholic Charities, and a reunion was arranged. Since the reunion, Betty said she has been much happier because the circle has been closed. She says she has a sense of something being finished and something being started. It was like something got fixed. Their relationship has been very open and very close, although Betty says, "We are still strangers to each other." They live three hundred miles apart, so seeing each other is not easy. Betty and her husband have no children, so Emma and her two children fill a void in their lives.

As Betty describes her birth daughter, it is obvious she is very unlike Betty. Emma is very confident, strong, has good self-esteem, and is spunky. Betty is thankful her daughter had such loving parents who made Emma feel wanted, loved, and special. To this day, Emma has not told her adoptive parents about her reunion with her birth mother because, as she says, "I don't want to hurt them."

At the time of our interview, the two had been reunited for eight years, and it appeared to be going smoothly. Two years after their reunion, Betty planned a large party for her family and friends to introduce Emma. Betty said it felt so strange to be so secretive for so many years, feeling like she was a woman with a "scarlet letter" and then to be shouting to the world that she has a birth daughter she had given up at birth. The guilt had vanished, and joy took its place. She wanted to share her joy with all those close to her.

This feeling of guilt dissolving and being replaced by relief and happiness is common with birth mothers after a reunion. It seems out of character that Betty, who appears to still be rather reserved and a bit meek, would want to plan a large party to celebrate her birth daughter. She said she could hardly wait for her family and friends to meet Emma.

Like so many other birth mothers, Betty gave birth to only one child. To be united with your one and only offspring is powerful.

When asked if she thought it would have been better if she'd been able to keep Emma, Betty struggled with the answer. She said that with no community or family help, she alone couldn't have given Emma the advantages and opportunities Emma had with her adoptive family. Betty also said she herself couldn't have gone to college if she had had a baby to support. Betty stated her depression would not have been healthy in raising a baby. So as traumatic as giving birth and the relinquishment of that baby were, Betty has been able to come to a peaceful conclusion that it all worked out as it should have.

Betty states that each time she and her daughter see each other, they become closer, although she adds, "We are still strangers to each other." She still feels a great sadness in not seeing Emma grow up.

Betty's life was dramatically changed because of her pregnancy. Her world became less secure as she became less secure. Therapy brought her back into the world of feelings again after she felt betrayed by the lack of support by the birth father as well as her parents. For well over twenty years, she struggled alone, afraid to put her trust in anyone. Fortunately, she now has a good marriage with a man who is understanding and does support her. She says he helps to take away the stigma of being an unwed mother.

Another birth mother we interviewed also talks about her guilt falling away. She tells the story of when she attended church with the adoptive parents of her son, who was forty years old at the time of their reunion. She had just met her birth son a few days earlier and was sitting in church on Sunday with the three of them when she was shocked to hear the minister announce, "We have a very special lady with us today. We all know the Smiths, and now I'd like to introduce John Smith's birth mother, Lydia, to all of you. Lydia, would you please stand up?"

Lydia said she wanted to disappear down a hole, certainly not stand up. After all these years of shame, for her pregnancy out of wedlock to be announced—in a church, of all places—was more than she could handle. She reluctantly stood up, and was further shocked to see the congregation smile and clap for her. Lydia said that at that moment, her years of shame and humiliation fell away.

Years ago, when young girls gave birth before marriage, their families and the professionals whom they worked with instilled such disgust and shame upon them that many carry that shame for the rest of their lives. A reunion can undo that feeling when you put a human being into the place of the pregnancy. How can you be ashamed of the human being you produced? Apparently, having it announced in church will also do the trick.

Rick Eckhardt, Birth Father

Rick – birth father
Becky – birth mother
Josie – their birth daughter

Rick was a nineteen-year-old college student when he was informed by his girlfriend that she was pregnant. He described their relationship as an "early college fling." They both agreed they could not keep their baby and considered going to Mexico for an abortion because it was not legal in the United States at the time. Becky later changed her mind, left college, and decided to continue her pregnancy. Becky and Rick broke off their relationship during this time, although both finally agreed that giving birth to the child was the right decision and adoption was the only route to pursue.

Rick's parents were not pleased when they were told of the situation and, in response to his telling them, sent him a package of condoms in the mail. Becky's parents were also upset with their daughter's pregnancy and were hostile toward Rick. Rick went to the hospital after Becky gave birth and was chased out of the hospital by Becky's angry father.

Rick and Becky have had an ongoing friendship throughout the years. They both agreed that they would not interfere in their daughter's life by searching her out, but they would more than welcome her into their lives if she searched for them. They made a point of keeping their contact information current with the adoption agency just in case.

They both carried on with their lives. Becky married another man, and Rick has had two marriages and two divorces. Both had subsequent children.

One day, Becky did get the phone call she and Rick both had been hoping for. The voice on the other end said, "I think I'm your birth daughter." Becky and Josie had a somewhat awkward and brief conversation that day, but further phone calls proved to be longer and friendlier. After a few months, Josie called Rick and went through a similar process. The three of them met at a restaurant eight months after the initial phone call.

Rick reports that their reunion was a wonderful experience and their ongoing relationship continues to be wonderful. He said that he and his family and Becky and her husband and children all attended Josie's wedding. At the time of our interview, Josie had one child, with another one on the way. Rick said everyone in all families involved appears to be "wonderful, open, and welcoming."

When asked if he felt their decision years ago had been the right one, Rick replied, "Absolutely. Given the same circumstances, we'd do it the same way again." Rick says getting to know Josie has been a mix of emotions for him. He sees her as his birth daughter and recognizes some genetic similarities, but also sees her as a stranger. He says, "We are all getting to know one another, and it's wonderful."

In this interview, we talked only with the birth father, Rick. He reported all throughout that everything was wonderful. He undoubtedly did go through some deep emotions along the way but said everything went smoothly. We didn't interview Becky, who may have had another version of this experience and undoubtedly might have reports of more emotional, perhaps traumatic, feelings as the birth mother. However, the reunion and subsequent mingling of families shows a mature attitude and acceptance of the reality it is.

Claire Reese, Birth Mother

Claire – birth mother
Curt – birth father
Kristi – their birth daughter

Claire is an example of a birth mother who searched and found her birth daughter, but her birth daughter doesn't want contact with Claire. Claire says she is able to live with this because, as she says, "Kristi was placed into a perfect family with perfect parents and perfect siblings. She's happy." Upon further conversation, it's obvious that Claire is not able to live with this as happily as she says. She lives with the sadness every day.

Claire met Curt in college, and they dated for a year before Claire became pregnant. Claire had not had sexual relations before Curt and was devastated when he said he wouldn't marry her. Even now, years later, Claire says Curt was the love of her life, even though she learned later that Curt impregnated two girls after Claire.

A local doctor pushed Claire into placing her child for adoption, telling her she had no other choice. Curt's parents and Claire's father wanted Claire to keep the baby, but the birth father and Claire's mother felt she should not. Claire was twenty-two years old at the time, but coming from a small Midwestern town in the 1960s, she would be a shamed woman if she returned home with a baby. Her daughter would also be labeled.

After finding Kristi, Claire said the anger she felt toward her mother and the birth father erupted in her. Without their input, she feels she would have kept her baby. Years later, when Claire and Curt met again, he told her he had had several divorces and wishes he would have married Claire and kept their baby.

While pregnant, Claire lived in a home for unwed mothers and, soon after returning to her own home, realized she couldn't stay there with her secret. She'd told none of her friends. She moved away, got a job, and met someone new—whom she married—and they had three sons.

Claire said her first pregnancy wasn't too much of an issue in her life although the fact that no one ever talked about it again was hard. Claire said she was too ashamed to bring up the subject, but burying her issues did have an effect on her later years. She felt having a baby and giving it up was unnatural.

Claire searched for her birth daughter and, upon finding her, contacted the adoptive parents first. They asked Kristi if she wanted to meet her birth mother. At first, Kristi said no, but then a week later, she called Claire and arranged a meeting without telling her adoptive parents. The two met one afternoon, and then that night met with Kristi's adoptive parents in their home. This was a surprise to Kristi's adoptive mother, and she was upset she had no prior warning about the meeting. The four of them took part in a very awkward evening. Communication between Claire and Kristi has been very sparse and strained ever since.

Claire said that after meeting with Kristi she was on an emotional roller coaster that was disruptive to her present family. She fluctuated between feeling elated and grieving for her lost child. Her youngest son was about twelve at the time and was afraid Claire would leave them all to go and live with Kristi. It took some time for Claire to come to grips with normalcy again.

Claire's sons were told of Kristi's existence, and although embarrassed for their mother at first, they have been supportive since. Claire met with Kristi just that one time, and her three younger sons have not met their older half-sister. One of them called Kristi a week after Claire and Kristi met but was met with coldness and an attitude of being intruded upon.

When asked how Claire felt about Kristi's attitude, Claire said she knows she has no right to Kristi, but her heart says she does. She thinks the reason for Kristi's coldness is that Kristi doesn't want to hurt her adoptive family, although Kristi told Claire that she thought she was unloved because Claire didn't keep her. This may be a lingering resentment.

Obviously, Claire is hurt by Kristi's rejection but laughs when she says Kristi doesn't need her because she's surrounded by her perfect family. At the time of Kristi's birth, Claire told no one, but once she found Kristi, she said she told everyone. Claire was expecting a warmer reaction than what she got, but she says now at least she's completed the circle. The emptiness in her is gone. She says she always carried around the feeling that she'd given birth to a child who had died, was lost to her.

At the time of her daughter's birth, one of the nurses offered to let Claire hold her baby, but Claire refused, knowing she emotionally couldn't handle it. This has always haunted her as a betrayal toward her daughter. She now says, "If I'd held her for a short time, maybe now she'd want me in her life."

Norma Hunter, Birth Mother

Norma – birth mother
Walter – birth father
Craig – birth son
Brenda – daughter of Norma and Walter, full sibling to Craig

Norma's interview was a very interesting one. She said she came from a long line of people who kept their emotions to themselves and didn't ask others for help. Her demeanor throughout the interview was one of sadness in relating her life. Her parents were in Europe during World War II and suffered greatly, but survived by being strong and lucky. After the war, they moved to the United States. Years later, Norma's unplanned pregnancy at age nineteen was not considered a tragedy. They'd seen enough of real tragedies in Europe during the war.

Norma said she was given full support from her parents and lived at home during her pregnancy. Her parents wanted her to ask one of her cousins to raise her child, but Norma decided against taking that path, and her parents never questioned her decision or tried to make her change her mind. During our interview, Norma came across as very strong, very realistic, and very wise. Several of our questions asked for an opinion about another person in her life, and Norma answered those questions with "I'm uncomfortable judging another person. You really never know their background and why they are doing what they're doing."

Norma and Walter knew each other all through high school and planned on getting married when Walter finished college. While in college, during his sophomore year, Walter was in a serious boating accident, and a severe head injury left him with diminished mental capacity. Doctors told the family he would never be normal again. It was at this very time that Norma discovered she was pregnant and also that she had a serious, perhaps terminal, illness. She wasn't sure she could carry her baby to its full term, but if she did, she knew she had to give it up for adoption. She couldn't count on either Walter or herself to be around as a parent. She wanted her baby to have every advantage she felt she could not provide as a single parent, potentially a single parent in poor health, if she survived at all. In hindsight, Norma says that if she had known her illness was to be cured, she would have kept her baby.

Norma sought help from a religious agency, which helped her with the process of giving birth and placing her child for adoption, but she paid a heavy price. Everyone she dealt with, from the social workers to the doctors, told her what a bad person she was for having sex before marriage. By the time they were through with her, Norma said her burden of guilt was almost more than she could bear. She constantly asked herself what kind of woman gives up her baby. This thought dominated her life for many years afterward. She knew she had ruined her own life, and probably her baby's life as well.

Several years after the birth of the baby, both Norma and Walter were in better health. Walter did recover significantly more than the doctors had predicted, and Norma's illness was cured. They started to see each other again and eventually married. Their marriage lasted eighteen years and produced a daughter, Brenda, eight years younger than Craig, the baby Norma had given up for adoption. Brenda and Craig were full siblings.

In hindsight, Norma says she married Walter because of her guilt. She didn't think she deserved happiness and married him as her "penance." Walter had recovered from his accident, but his head injury changed his personality, and he became verbally and emotionally abusive. Norma thought she deserved this, but her daughter didn't, and often told her mother she should leave her abusive marriage. When Brenda was ten, Norma divorced Walter. Brenda and Norma became a family of two and were unusually close.

Norma desperately wanted to know of the son she had relinquished but felt she had no right to intrude into his life. She loved Brenda but missed her son. Norma just hoped and prayed that one day she would get the magic phone call that would lead to their reunion.

Craig had been thinking about searching for his birth family for years, but it wasn't until his midthirties that he followed through. He was thirty-five when Norma got a phone call that her birth son wanted to meet her.

Norma said she had a flurry of emotions—from anger at herself to euphoria—before their meeting. She was given a letter that Craig had written to his then-unknown birth mother, saying he would like to meet her. Norma said she put the letter down and told Brenda what area of town Craig lived in, where he went to college, and what his major was. None of this was stated in the letter, and all of it turned out to be accurate. When asked how she knew, Norma said she just had a "knowing."

Their initial meeting was all that initial meetings should be. There were many tears from both of them, some of sadness and some of joy, and hour upon hour (ten in all) of talking nonstop. Craig was at the meeting place first, and when Norma approached him, they hugged for a long time, and then Craig put his hand on Norma's abdomen and said, "This is where I came from."

At the time of our interview, they had been reunited for four years. The relationship Norma and Craig have is very successful, but not everyone in their families can say the same. Craig's adoptive mother has struggled greatly, knowing Craig now shares much of his life with Norma. Since the reunion, his adoptive mother feels her relationship with Craig has been threatened. Brenda, at first, loved the idea of having a big brother, but that was short-lived. Her jealousy has been a powerful factor in their newly reunited family.

Norma told her daughter, even before meeting Craig, that for a while, Craig would probably be the focus of her life. Brenda said she understood this and would be supportive. After a few months, Brenda realized she was no longer number one in her mother's life and she had been replaced by Craig. Norma admits she doesn't know how to handle this, and when either of them comes to her to complain about the other, Norma tells them they need to keep her out of it and settle it between themselves.

Craig has much in common with Norma, much more than he has in common with his adoptive parents, when it comes to interests and lifestyle. Norma says Craig and Brenda both have similar strong personalities.

Norma says she no longer lives with guilt and is grateful every day that Craig is now in her life. Craig has found a kindred soul in finding his birth mother. They share interests in the theater, classical music, opera, cooking, and many other things.

Norma says Brenda is now married and has her own independent life and is getting along a little better with Craig. Craig's adoptive parents still feel sad that they couldn't provide for Craig what his birth mother can now, the interests and commonalities.

Even though other family members are struggling with the new family dynamics, Norma and Craig are much happier, and both feel complete. Craig's feeling of emptiness has disappeared, and Norma's strong feelings of guilt and unworthiness have also disappeared. These have been replaced in both by gratitude that two kindred souls now know each other. Norma said her pregnancy and relinquishment have had a profound effect on her life. She is now more compassionate, open-minded, accepting, and understanding of others. "You never know what other people are going through," she said. "We all need to be respectful of other people's baggage."

Henry Lee, Birth Father

Henry – birth father
Valerie – birth mother

Henry was twenty-six years old when his daughter was born, but he didn't know he had a daughter until three years later. That has had a great effect on his daily life. On his computer, he has a picture of his birth daughter, taken at the time of her birth. He looks at her every day.

He and the birth mother had been dating for about six months before they became intimate. That was the first and last time because shortly thereafter, Valerie refused to see Henry. Valerie went to live with an aunt at that time, and Henry was received coldly and harshly by Valerie's aunt. He was told that no one in their family wanted to see Henry ever again. Henry was confused since he didn't know the reason was that Valerie was pregnant.

Three years later, he found out he was a birth father. He was further distraught when he learned that his daughter had been placed for adoption immediately after her birth. Henry tracked down Valerie and asked why she had never told him she was pregnant. Henry had a good steady job and said he would have married Valerie, and together, they would have provided a good home for their daughter. Valerie stated that at the time, she was disgusted with both herself and Henry and wanted nothing to do with him.

Henry looks at the picture of their daughter taken the day she was born and realizes she is now an adult. Henry says he misses her every day. He said he has never searched because she was placed in a closed adoption, and he doesn't have any information to help him start looking.

Henry was very passionate about wanting to know his daughter, and fears he will die before that ever happens. He says he comes from a large, strong family and wants to share that with his daughter. This birth has changed Henry's life by providing a daily sadness that he feels he is helpless to overcome. He's frustrated that for three years he was never told he had a daughter, and he is now frustrated with a system that prevents him from possibly ever knowing her.

The interviewers had no doubt that Henry would have been a conscientious father dedicated to building a strong family. Henry mentioned several times that his own mother was also saddened that Henry would never know his daughter and that she would never know her granddaughter. She was very sympathetic toward Henry's situation.

The birth mother was not unlike other birth mothers who never told birth fathers of their pregnancies and, thus, never gave birth fathers the chance to keep their babies. In this case, Valerie didn't want to marry Henry.

Often, birth fathers are perceived as not wanting to be involved with the children they create. However, a few of the birth fathers we talked with had an even stronger desire to keep their birth children than many birth mothers did. They often didn't know of the baby's existence for a short time, and by the time they found out they were a birth father, their baby had already been adopted. They didn't endure the months of pregnancy like the birth mother, who was involved in making life-changing decisions. The shock of finding out after the fact seemed to still affect them.

Henry says he is as devastated today as he was the day he found out he had fathered a daughter. He feels passionately that she should have been raised within his family that he proudly says is large and dynamic. He hates the fact that his daughter will never know of her heritage and be able to live among her biological relatives. He wants to find her and introduce her to her family history and says he is terrified he will never find her.

SECTION IV

11

Adoptive Parents

Below is a sampling of the questions asked of adoptive parents:

- Do you have biological children as well as adopted children?
- Did you have miscarriages? How did you react? Did you feel like you had lost a child?
- Was it a relatively comfortable process going through adoption interviews, home studies, etc.? How did adoption professionals treat you?
- Did you feel adoption workers were sensitive to your miscarriages or inability to become pregnant? Were you made to feel different because you could not conceive or carry a fetus to term?
- Did you have misgivings about adopting, raising another person's baby with different genes and hereditary issues?
- Did you think you could overcome any issues with love?

- Did both you and your spouse feel the same way about the decision to adopt?
- How did your family and friends react to your plans to adopt? Did their reaction affect you?
- What were your feelings when you first saw your child? How did you view your child after a few months? A few years?
- How long did it take to feel that your adopted baby was "your" child, belonged to only you, and that it was meant to be?
- Were there times when you viewed your child as different from the biological members of your family?
- Did you try to mold your child to be like other family members, or did you see him as a unique individual and raise him with that attitude?
- How important was it that your child fit into your family?
- Did you ever feel disappointed in your child and think if he were biological things would be different? Were there ever times you thought that a biological child of yours would act differently than your adopted child?
- Were there times you missed this biological link?
- Did your child share family interests in academics, athletics, etc.? If not, was this a disappointment? How did you handle this?
- How old was your child when you told him/her they were adopted? How often did you discuss adoption? How often did you discuss your child's birth parents?
- How often did your child ask about adoption or birth parents?
- Would you describe your child as having more anger issues than normal?
- Did you ever think your child was grieving for his lost family?
- Do you think your child believed he was truly a part of your family, that he fit in?
- As a teenager, do you feel he felt like an outsider and separated himself from family activities?

- Did you think you had to emphasize a family feeling of love and loyalty more so than if you'd had only biological children? Did you work at making everyone feel you were one family?
- Did your child ever say, "You are not my mother [or father]"? Did he ever say he didn't have to go by your rules because he wasn't a part of your family?
- Do you think your child struggled with not knowing who he was, with identity issues, or wondering where he belonged?
- In hindsight, if you could go back, would you still adopt?
- How has adoption changed your life?

We found it interesting that all adoptive parents stated emphatically that they were their child's true parent. They could not conceive of anyone else loving their child more than they did. It was almost a frightening thought to them, and they felt that if their child had been in another family, he would not have been understood and not been loved as intensely. This statement came out in answer to the last couple of questions in the interview. In some families, there were years of trying to maintain a loving cohesive family while facing rebellion and rejection from their adopted children. Still, all parents stated, emotionally at times, that they were the only parents who could love and understand their child. In reading the following interviews, the reader might see in some of the stories just how remarkable that statement is.

12

Adoptive-Parent Profiles

Nina Taber, Adoptive Parent and Adoptee

Nina Taber has a lot of experience with adoption. She is an adoptee, an adoptive parent, and is currently a social worker working in the adoption field. But her life is more complicated than that.

Nina lived with her parents and three older siblings until the age of five, when her parents divorced. At that time, her father gained custody of the children and moved to another city, where he placed his four children in the care of his sister. They remained there for two years before being placed in an orphanage. Nina was seven at this time. When Nina was eleven and her sister was twelve, the two of them were adopted together by a couple. Nina's older brothers elected not to be adopted as they were teenagers at this time, so they lived in foster care until they went out on their own.

Nina and her sister were the only children of her adoptive parents. Her adoptive father was a heavy drinker and very domineering within the family. He sexually abused Nina starting six months after the adoption, and this continued until Nina was fourteen, when she finally told her mother. Soon after this, he dramatically held a gun to his head and threatened to kill himself in front of the children. Outside the home, her father was considered to be a well-respected man, and Nina says she cringes every time someone says something complimentary about him, since she knows the type of man he truly was.

Nina is an outgoing, cheerful individual. She says her life at the orphanage was positive, that it was strict, but there were loving people there to care for her. Her adoptive parents were difficult to deal with. Her sexual abuse was traumatic. Her adoptive mother also was dominated by her husband and spent her life trying to pacify him.

Nina married when she was in her early twenties, and she and her husband had a daughter who tragically was killed in a car accident when she was two years old. Nina wanted to try to get pregnant again even though the doctors said she could not. From this time on, Nina's husband was very committed to adopting, and eventually, Nina agreed. They had a positive experience with the adoption process itself, and even though they experienced challenges with their sons, she is very positive about her situation.

Her sons were twenty and twenty-six at the time of the interview. The older son had been rebellious in his late teen years and wandered for several years, not keeping in touch with his family except for two or three phone calls a year. At twenty-one, he came back, lived at home, and went to college, agreeing to abide by the family rules of no drugs, alcohol, etc.

Their younger son was diagnosed with severe attention deficit disorder (ADD) at the age of seven. Even though he is an extremely bright boy, his educational years have been a challenge due to his ADD. For most of the boys' lives, Nina has worked for an adoption agency, and this, coupled with her own childhood experiences, has enabled Nina to be more realistic than many adoptive parents. She has a broader perspective because of her personal experiences.

From the beginning, she has sent pictures and letters to the agency who placed her sons in the hope that the birth mothers would ask about them. Indeed, that happened, and Nina received information back about the birth mothers and their lives. She shared this with her sons. It wasn't until the boys were in their early twenties, however, that they actually met their birth mothers. This has been a good experience for all involved. Nina's older son is very close to a daughter of his birth mother since they share much in common and look very much alike. He has more contact with her than with his birth mother.

This interview was one of the longest we conducted. We saw tears from Nina only twice during the interview. The first time was very shortly into the interview, when she spoke of her biological daughter who was killed at age two. The second time was almost at the end of the interview, when she spoke of being at her aunt's (birth father's sister's) funeral. Nina was forty-five at the time, and a cousin (son of the deceased aunt) came up to her to tell Nina that his mother wanted to adopt Nina and her siblings at the time of the divorce (when Nina was five) and that his mother cried for weeks afterward because this was not possible. Nina feels that in retaliation for the way her aunts and uncles shunned her birth father, he declared that no relatives could adopt his children. She cried upon hearing at age forty-five, for the first time, that there was a dear woman who wanted to love and raise her. How different her life would have been.

Nina is unique in that her whole life has been involved with disruption in families. She is a very religious woman and a very strong woman. She feels that events in life happen for a purpose. In looking back at her life, she recognizes her loss issues but doesn't appear to let them define her. The loss of her birth parents, the loss of innocence due to sexual abuse as a child, and eventually the loss of her biological daughter are all very dramatic and traumatic events. Just one in a person's lifetime could be shattering.

Nina's job deals with the issue of loss in working with birth parents, adoptive parents, and adopted children. She certainly can relate to all sides of adoption. Perhaps working on a daily basis with this makes her own personal situation more common in her mind, thus enabling her to accept it as a part of her life.

Growing up first in her aunt's house, and later in the orphanage, Nina had some contact with aunts, uncles, and cousins who would visit occasionally. They included Nina and her siblings on their vacations several times. She said this was essential in keeping her grounded as to her identity. She liked these good people, and even though they could not adopt her, she had enough contact with them to realize they were loving family members.

After the adoption of her two sons, Nina wanted to provide this same advantage for them, and said that was why she continued to send letters and pictures of her sons to be put in the birth mothers' files in the adoption agency. Nina feels strongly that all adopted children need this link to their biological past to feel continuity in their existence. When asked about passing along negative facts about birth parents, Nina answered that at the proper age and in a loving way, this can be spoken of since it is a part of the child's past.

Her overall demeanor is one of empathy for all people and an interest in all people. She says she loves learning, and it appears that working with people is one unique way to learn about life and the people in it. She certainly has had enough life experiences to understand people. This encompassing appreciation of life and all it offers is a benefit for those she touches, and her job of supporting all in the adoption triad is undoubtedly ongoing therapy for her.

Karen and Warren Grant, Adoptive Parents

Karen – adoptive mother
Warren – adoptive father
Dorothy – adopted daughter
Emily – adopted daughter

Karen and Warren have both biological and adopted children. The uniqueness of the Grant family is that they adopted two children before deciding to produce their two biological children. Their adoption experience had no connection to infertility issues. They decided, as a young married couple, that they wanted to adopt children who needed a home. The Grant's, who are white, did not want to adopt Caucasian children because they felt they wanted to provide a home for children who, because of their race, might be hard to place.

Their first adopted daughter was biracial (a white birth mother and black birth father), and their second adopted daughter was Chinese. They adopted Dorothy when they were married just one year, and Emily was adopted two years later. Their two biological sons arrived four and eight years after that. Their adoptions were in the early seventies, when there was still a movement by some to block transracial adoptions.

Both of their extended families were unhappy when they heard of the Grant's plan for a family. This disappointed Karen and Warren. Since the Grant's lived in several different cities while their children were growing up, this concern on the part of their extended family was not a present daily issue for them.

Race was an issue for Dorothy. She is biracial but prefers to be considered black. She searched for her birth parents but only wanted to find her black father, and wasn't interested in finding her white birth mother. During her childhood, she said that she really wanted to be with more black people. The Grant's made a point of living in an integrated neighborhood and going to an integrated church, but Dorothy's daily homelife was in her white family.

Emily felt more isolated than Dorothy because there were very few Asian children in her school or neighborhood. She didn't appear to be as preoccupied with being a different race than her parents as much as Dorothy did. Both did return to their roots in choosing a marriage partner: Dorothy married a black man, and Emily married a Chinese man.

Karen said that raising her two biological sons was ever so much easier than her first two children. She saw the work of genetics at work. The personalities and needs of her adopted children were very different from those of her biological sons. Overall, there were no serious problems within the family, and the four children, who now are grown with families of their own, are very close.

Karen said that it seems to her that her two oldest seemed to need her more and are somewhat dysfunctional in their adult lives. Her two biological sons appear to sail along smoothly while Karen says her oldest two always seem to be in some traumatic drama where they are the star.

Karen offered that she thought some adopted children may think their parents owe them more and for a longer time frame. Karen says she thinks some are manipulative with their parents, perhaps thinking, "You plucked me out and set me down in this family. Now you are responsible for me." Karen says both her adopted children put "guilt trips" on her and have for some time. They complained that they lived in the wrong neighborhood, they didn't fit in with other kids, they didn't like the schools they attended, etc.

Another theory for this apparent neediness could be that some adopted children/adults want to make sure they still "belong" to their families, and so may not develop the necessary skills to be absolutely independent. As long as parents are still needed, the children still have a place to go for help. Does this keep the connection strong in a situation where the child/adult may think the connection may break? Contacting parents with a need certainly keeps the family connection active.

Karen and Warren adopted at a time when international adoptions were beginning to be more visible in our society. Transracial adoptions were controversial for a period, but they, too, were occurring more often. The Grant's were caught up in the spirit of it all: providing a loving home for children who might not have that opportunity. Even though they lived in several cities during their young married years, Karen said that the first thing she always did after each move was seek out an adoption support group, and those people became her friends. Her children were surrounded by other adopted children, and Karen found it comfortable to be with other adoptive families who had similar challenges. It wasn't until after their two biological children were born that Karen realized what a challenging job she had with her first two children. As she looks back now, she realizes just how much they all went through.

Her two older children struggled with identity issues throughout their lives. People stared at them on the streets and asked them about their multicolored family. This became tiresome after a while.

Karen expressed that she's learned over the years that some things cannot be changed. There are some characteristics of her adopted children that she would like to change, but she now knows that genetics are stronger than her desires. She says she has become more realistic and accepting. She adds, "There are some qualities of your children you just learn to live with."

Pat and Frank Reed, Adoptive Parents

Pat – adoptive mother
Frank – adoptive father
Fritz – adopted son
Bill – adopted son
Nicky – adopted daughter

There are many adoptive families in which the search for birth families is not a big issue. If anything, it may be only an annoyance to all within the family. The Reed family falls into this category. Pat and Frank Reed have three adopted children—Fritz, Bill, and Nicky. They are a close, strong family who have weathered some storms and come through them successfully.

Both of the sons were on drugs during their teen years. These were turbulent years for the family, testing the very strength of their bonds. Both boys are now recovering drug addicts, thanks to professional residential long-term help and strong, supportive parents. Both boys are now adults with families, and the world would call them successful. Their daughter, Nicky, is one of those young ladies that everyone loves. She is kind, loving, personable, and genuine. She also now has her own family and a loving marriage.

None of the adopted Reed children want to search for their birth parents and, in fact, are offended by the very suggestion. Both boys were located by their birth mothers during their teen years. The birth mothers sent cards, letters, and made phone calls to Fritz and Bill, and the whole Reed family looked upon this as an offensive intrusion into their closely knit family. Both Bill and Fritz became so upset when their birth mothers made contact with them that Pat started setting their birthday cards aside until after the birthdays were over so the boys wouldn't be upset by receiving a card from their birth mothers. Pat was tired of the negative and angry reactions from her boys, and thought the birth mothers didn't have the right to upset her sons.

Now that their children are adults and have their own lives, there is much visiting back and forth and frequent phone calls. One of their sons even bought the house next door to his parents after he'd been married for ten years. All of the children have children, and there is frequent ongoing contact among family members.

When asked about searching, the three children said they love their close family and are complete in their identity. There may be an issue with both boys fearing that their birth parents were addicts, since addiction can run in families and the tendency can be inherited. Bill's birth mother wrote an initial long letter to him, telling him that she had three other children, all with different fathers. When Bill compared this possible existence versus the secure, loving family that is his, one can understand his reluctance to have contact with his birth mother.

There are many adoptees who say that every adoptee is a searcher, but some are afraid to get started. There are other adoptees who say they are secure with their identity and the family they have. They see no logic in threatening this wonderful situation. These adoptees enjoy a close and supportive relationship with their parents and have no desire to revisit the past or their biological origins. It could be fear of what they will find or loyalty to what they have, but the fact is that in their minds, their identity is cemented within their adoptive family. They are not only content with this stance but also are very happy. All members of the Reed family would agree on this. They like their family just the way it is.

Betty and Ted Gilmore, Adoptive Parents

Betty – adoptive mother
Ted – adoptive father
Fran – adopted daughter
Jean – adopted daughter

The vast majority of adoptive families, even though they have additional challenges to work through, are happy and successful. However, the whole world seems to hear of the exceptions. The Gilmore's are one of those exceptions.

The Gilmore's adopted two daughters. Their older daughter, Fran, is greatly insulted when she is asked to talk about searching for her birth family. She is extremely close to her parents, and the thought of anyone else intruding in this close relationship is offensive to her. She says, "I've seen a lot of families while growing up, and I've never seen one better than mine. I love my family, and they love me. I'm in charge of what I do with my life and finding out some biological information, some of which could be negative, is of no interest to me at all."

Their younger daughter, Jean, was conceived by rape. Her birth mother and her birth grandmother were both incapacitated by mental illness. This information was not conveyed to the Gilmore's at the time of her placement within their family. Crime seemed to be a way of life for Jean's birth father and his family. Most served some time in prison, and her birth father is currently serving a life sentence in prison. Unfortunately, Jean followed in their footsteps and spent some time in prison as well.

Jean's birth mother called the adoptive family when Jean was about thirty years old and in prison. At that time, the birth mother informed them of the birth parents' situations. She was almost afraid to ask about the outcome of her birth daughter, and was not surprised to hear of the years of turmoil and Jean's prison sentence.

Ted called the adoption agency to ask why they had not been told of Jean's heritage. The adoption agency said they did not know and apologized to the Gilmores for the situation, but they can never take away the heartache and anger over the frustrations the Gilmores struggled with for years. Their survival philosophy gives them some solace, knowing that they kept Jean safe during her life up until her late teens. "That was perhaps our purpose all along," Betty said. "We just didn't know it. We were helping her to be so much more than she was ever capable of being."

The Gilmores spent thousands of dollars on therapy and psychiatrist's bills. Jean has a limited IQ, but was placed in a family of achieving college graduates, who were given no background on her potential limitations. Their goals for their daughter were unrealistic, but they didn't know that.

The question then becomes this: would it have helped Jean to know her birth father was a psychopath and she was conceived by rape? This is the nightmare scenario that some adoptees fear but are reassured by others that it's never true. In Jean's case, it is true. The question the Gilmores faced when they found this out in later years was whether this information would help their daughter. They chose not to share this information with Jean, thinking it would only hinder her more in her quest for any chance of a decent life.

The Gilmores have a unique situation. They are unusually close to Fran, now in her late thirties, and can't imagine life without their daughter, but they also are angered by an adoption system that would place a baby with a potentially harmful genetic background into their family. The crowning blow came when Jean, at the age of twenty-four, physically attacked her mother. After all the years of trying to get Jean the help she needed, after the thousands of dollars spent on therapy and thousands of tears shed on Jean's behalf, the family had to return to a safe and sane place. Jean was asked to leave the house.

There has been intermittent communication since, but the family is afraid of Jean's violent nature. At the time of the interview, Jean had been out of prison for several years and appeared to be trying to live a good life. She had a steady job and was doing well.

Betty and Ted offered a world to Jean that she could not embrace. Her low IQ and any harmful genetic material she inherited from her birth parents blocked her partaking of the benefits of being part of a loving, generous, achieving family. This was not only unfair to her parents and sister but also very unfair to Jean to be exposed to a life she couldn't grasp. It was beyond her reach.

Denise and Colin Goodwin, Adoptive Parents

Denise – adoptive mother
Colin – adoptive father
Laura – adopted daughter
Tad – adopted son

What if you were a young couple sitting in an adoption worker's office, and the adoption worker told you that over the years you'd spend countless hours in therapists' offices? You'd deal with learning disabilities, uncontrollable behavior, sexual abuse, children dropping out of high school, unplanned pregnancies, and visiting children in prison. During our interview with a couple who did have to face all these issues with their children, they were asked, "Knowing what you know now, would you still have adopted?" One would expect both parents to say no. That was not the case.

Denise, the mother, who was at home dealing with all these issues, did say no at first. Colin's answer was, "Yes, even with all the problems. I figured if we'd had biological kids, they might have caused problems too. This is what parenting is all about." Denise, having second thoughts, added, "Well, if we hadn't adopted, we wouldn't have these wonderful grandchildren now, so I guess I'd have to change my answer and say yes too."

Ten years ago, when both their son and daughter were teenagers, their attitudes were very different than during our current interview. Colin was very angry that life had dealt him this hand. Denise was trying to keep body and soul together while navigating a life very foreign to their background. They had no experience in drugs, learning disabilities, jails, and mental problems that caused uncontrollable behavior. They sought help from the beginning and had therapy for their children for years, but it wasn't very helpful. For the most part, they were on their own, struggling with issues unfamiliar to them.

Neither of their children, Laura and Tad, has searched for their birth parents. Denise and Colin passed along all the information they were told about their birth parents, but it wasn't very much. Tad expresses hate for his birth mother and says he never wants to see her. Laura is perplexed as to why her birth mother kept her full brother and sister but placed her for adoption as an infant. She'd like to meet her siblings but says she doesn't want to meet her birth mother. The Goodwins told both children they would help them search for their birth parents when they reached the age when they could do it legally. At this point, neither has the desire to search.

Denise said that for years, she was very perplexed. "I couldn't figure it out. I was doing all the same things the other mothers were doing, but they had good kids, and my kids were in trouble. They were always angry. I didn't know what I was doing wrong. We were all raising our children the same way, but our results were very different. We were told when we adopted them as babies to just take them home and forget they were adopted. No one told us about adoption issues. Even therapists and counselors didn't mention adoption issues. No wonder the therapy wasn't successful."

Ten years later, during our current interview, Colin and Denise presented a different perspective on their life. Now their children were in their late twenties; their daughter, Laura, was a single parent, raising three children from two different fathers, and they hadn't had contact with their son, Tad, for eight years. Adoptive parents would not wish for either of these situations.

During the interview, both Colin and Denise told the story of their family unemotionally, very factually. All the pain was masked and set aside. They appeared to be mellow, factual, accepting of their situation. Their relationship with their daughter is now very close. Laura expresses her love for her parents and realizes now all that they have gone through. Laura tells her mother, "It's too bad you couldn't have biological children because then you wouldn't have had all these problems."

Colin and Denise love their grandchildren, and they, in a way, have a happier family now than they have ever had. Laura has problems but has learned to cope and compensate for them. Tad is out of their lives, at least for the present time. Life is smoother and calmer than it has been for years. They are appreciating the good that is left.

Denise and Colin said for years they had heavy guilt concerning their children but now realize they did a very good job, considering the circumstances. They now know their son suffers from the results of alcohol fetal syndrome, undiagnosed while he was a boy. They now know their daughter suffered the results of learning disabilities and sexual abuse. The Goodwins had these issues to deal with, along with adoption issues, all at a time in our society when very little was known about these problems.

In looking back, both parents agree that they did a wonderful job even though for years they thought otherwise. They now have the perspective of time and the advantage of a society enlightened about all their issues. They say, "Things may not have turned out too well, but we think we saved their lives. Who knows what would have happened to them if they had been in another family? We put good things into our children. They know good values, and it's up to them to accept them or not. Laura is a wonderful mother. She's been able to hold down a job for four years now. We feel good about ourselves."

In looking back, Denise says, "I used to be naïve. I thought love could conquer all, but now I know that isn't true. We had no idea, nor did the therapists, of what we had been given to handle. It was tough. We had many unhappy years, and I do feel cheated that I missed so much. We never went to a high school graduation. We never saw our kids go to a prom dance. Our kids had so many problems that the good part of their childhood was overshadowed. We did things as a family, like take trips, played games and sports together, but the problems were always there. We tried to be a normal family, but we weren't."

The interview revealed that the Goodwins appeared to do everything right according to the current view of parenting. They told their children from the beginning that they were adopted, they tried to raise them like they had been raised, and they tried to live their lives like every other good, solid family. The Goodwins were loving, dedicated parents.

The glaring error in their lives was the same glaring error that most adoptive families share. They were never told about adoption issues their children would face. In fact, they were told by society that there was no such thing as an adoption issue, and yes, that love could conquer all. Denise, now through her work in dealing with young adoptive parents, is in a position to explain adoption issues to them. She is helping the future generation of adoptive parents, hoping they can avoid the experiences of the Goodwin family.

In looking back, both Colin and Denise say their life was like a roller coaster, and they couldn't get off. They now say their steadfastness produced what success they now enjoy. In this case, one could say that the adoption was successful, but that doesn't necessarily say the adopted children were successful—at least society would not say so. Parents can do all the right things, but if they can't get a diagnosis and help for the suspected genetic problems their children bring with them to the family, the children are going to suffer. There will be a lasting legacy of issues. As the children grow into adulthood, they can see that their parents were loving and dedicated but lacked the knowledge to help them deal with their genetic issues.

There are other families like the Goodwins. We would like to hope that there was more help for these families, but the reality is many of these families were on their own. It is a tribute to all members of these families to see how they have come through their years of turbulence. For instance, Denise can earnestly say that her daughter is a very good mother. Where did she learn these skills? Laura learned these mothering skills from her mother, Denise. Both Denise and Colin are dedicated grandparents to Laura's children. Laura is their daughter, and they love her. Were Tad to come back into their lives, they would still warily receive him back.

There are people in our society who think that when adopted children portray very bad antisocial behavior, it would be natural for adoptive parents to throw up their hands and cut off the relationship. Disruption can happen both in adoptive, as well as biological, families. However, in many situations where children have brought discord and turbulence into their families, we see over and over how compassionate adoptive parents can be, how steadfast they are in loving their children.

As they grow into adulthood, if children can understand what their situation was and what their parents endured, they are often inordinately close to their parents. The family has been through years of hardship, but they are a family, and many adoptive parents say, "Of course, they will always be our children, no matter what they've done. If we turn our backs on them, they will have no one. We belong together." Society should look upon this compassion and forgiveness (on the part of both parents and children) as an example of character, the kind of strong character the adoption agency hopes for when they place children in adoptive families.

Nicole and Ken Parker, Adoptive Parents

Nicole – adoptive mother
Ken – adoptive father
Larry – adopted son
Patty – adopted daughter

The interview regarding adoption was very short-lived with this family. When asked if her children, Larry and Patty, had ever shown any interest in searching, Nicole's answer was "Of course not!" She went on to say, "We are our children's parents—always have been, always will be. We've had financial struggles all our life. We've never owned a house, always rented, but even though our house situation wasn't always solid, our family was rock solid."

Larry's birth mother traveled a thousand miles to Iowa in order to give birth there and have her baby adopted by a Midwestern family. They know very little about Patty's birth family, but Patty always said she wasn't interested in finding them. She knew who her family was.

Nicole says she has always been a high-energy person, and her energy went into her family. She added, "They all knew I'd give up my life for them in a heartbeat. We've moved a lot, and we couldn't be closer, even now that they're grown. Ken and I have known each other since the sixth grade. We dated all through high school, and we've been married almost forever. We stick together as a family. We're there for each other, no matter what."

Their son, Larry, was working in South America for some time, and he'd make a point of seeing his parents every time he came back to the United States to go to the home office, even though his parents weren't on his travel route. This was several times a year, and Nicole and Ken really appreciated it. Larry later divorced, and his visits home were more frequent and longer in duration. Nicole said she knew he needed them more then.

A few years ago, when Patty's husband's company transferred him, she told her husband, "I'm not moving 1,200 miles away from my parents. One day soon, they'll be old, and when they get sick, I want to be there to take care of them." So three months after they moved their family, they bought a little house for Ken and Nicole a mile from theirs. They were still together as a family.

When asked about her children's birth parents, Nicole answered, "Birth parents? I can't imagine where they'd fit into this tight family. The four of us have been whole and complete from the beginning. Ken and I have been blessed in finding each other in this life and then in having Larry and Patty as children. We couldn't have asked for greater kids. Larry had a lot of health problems from the beginning, but those were the only problems we had with them. We loved them desperately, and they turned out to be wonderful kids."

Ken has always been less talkative than his wife. When the interviewer turned to him, he smiled and said, "Amen. What more is there to say?"

Trudy and Chuck Clark, Adoptive Parents

Trudy – adoptive mother
Chuck – adoptive father
Nancy – adopted daughter
Meg – adopted daughter
Hank – Meg's husband
Hans – Nancy's significant other

When a young couple is standing at the altar of marriage, they are anticipating a wonderful life ahead. They anticipate children and a happy family life. Sometimes, when this same couple looks back on thirty or forty years of marriage, they find it hard to believe what they have not only survived but also weathered beautifully. The

Clarks are one of those couples. Trudy and Chuck are your typical salt-of-the-earth, down-home, ordinary type of people. There are many adjectives to describe the kind of people they are, but it all boils down to quiet, likeable, loyal, solid.

Trudy had a stillborn baby and four miscarriages before they looked to adoption to complete their family. They adopted two girls who were infants when adopted. Their young lives were happy and fairly normal, but then Chuck was transferred by his company two thousand miles out to the West Coast.

At the time, Nancy was eighteen and starting art school, and Meg was still in high school, soon to be sixteen years old. A week after their move, Meg's boyfriend showed up and convinced Meg to sneak out of her window at night and drive two thousand miles with him back to where she used to live. Trudy and Chuck were shocked that their almost sixteen-year-old daughter would take such a drastic step. Meg was determined to stay with Hank, so they moved in with his grandmother.

Both of them dropped out of high school and got jobs at minimum wage. At seventeen, they were still together, so Chuck and Trudy reluctantly gave their permission for Meg to marry. At eighteen, Meg had a baby; at nineteen, she had another baby; and at twenty-four, she had her last baby. All were sons. Throughout all those years, whenever Chuck had a vacation, he and Trudy drove two thousand miles to be with Meg and her family. Trudy says they bought clothes for the whole family, stocked their freezer with food, and painted and made repairs around their small rented house. Then they drove two thousand miles back home.

Meg and Hank struggled financially for years, but by his midthirties, Hank had been successful in business. And it appeared to be a good marriage. When their sons were the same age as they were when they ran away to be together, Meg and Hank were appalled at what they had done years earlier. They were also surprised that they survived it all. Hank had little family, but Meg's family was always available for them, even though this was not what they foresaw as they were standing at the altar years before.

Years later, when Hank was in his forties, he was arrested for fraudulent practices in his what appeared to be successful business. Meg discovered there had been many lies throughout their years, and while Hank was in prison, she divorced him. When Hank eventually got out of prison, their family was split in their loyalties. Hank told lies about Meg to their sons in hopes of gaining their sympathy and loyalty. The two older sons knew what Hank was doing and wanted nothing to do with him, but the younger son, at the age of twelve, insisted on living with his father. Hank harassed Meg and his other two sons for several years afterward. During this time, Trudy and Chuck provided the security Meg and her boys needed, both psychologically and financially. A few years later, Meg met and married a wonderful man, and steadiness and love came back into their fractured family.

Nancy was the Clark's older daughter. She had some health problems, but they were corrected by a series of operations when Nancy was in her teens. Nancy was always her own person. She was an artist who painted and sculpted and made jewelry, in addition to being a singer and a model. The challenge in living with Nancy was that her artist's talents emerged at night. She would sleep all day and work all night. The family would often pass each other in the kitchen about six o'clock or seven o'clock in the morning just as Trudy, Chuck, and Meg were getting ready for the day—and Nancy was about to go to bed for the day.

One day, while Nancy was in her early twenties, she was contacted by the adoption agency that placed her. The message was that her birth father wanted to have contact with her, but the agency advised Nancy to contact her half-sisters first before contacting him. Nancy hadn't thought much about searching, and actually didn't do anything for several months. When she did phone her half-sisters, they both advised her strongly to stay away from her birth father. They said he was a violent man who had a drinking problem. This was enough for Nancy to end any thoughts of a reunion with either the birth father or her half-sisters.

After Nancy finished art school, she went to Europe for more study. While there, she met a young musician, Hans, and fell in love. Nancy lived in Europe for fifteen years. Trudy and Chuck went to Europe almost every year for a three- to four-week visit with Nancy, and every second year, Nancy and Hans would come to visit in the United States for a month. Nancy lived as the stereotypical bohemian-style artist. She had different color hair—we're talking green, red, or blue—and wore vintage clothes, mainly black. Nancy was a beautiful girl and often modeled when she needed extra money. She was a fascinating, delightful, loving individual.

In her early thirties, she started a job in a community center in the inner city in Paris, working with underprivileged children, hoping to awaken their creativity. They regularly put on plays and art shows. Nancy was loved by the children and often became the surrogate encouraging big sister or mother figure for them.

Several years ago, while taking a group of these children on a two-week summer outing into the countryside, Nancy was killed instantly in a car accident. It was a shock for Trudy and Chuck to believe that their daughter—who was such a vital, free-spirited person—could actually be dead. Hans was equally devastated. Trudy and Chuck always felt close to Hans, and their broken hearts broke even more for him. Hans came to the United States for Nancy's funeral and then took some of Nancy's ashes back to Paris, the place where he and Nancy had lived her whole albeit short adult life. So Nancy's ashes are both here with the parents she loved and who loved her, and also with Hans, the love of her life and the man who adored her.

A few months after the funeral, the Clarks felt compelled to let Nancy's birth mother know of Nancy's premature death at age thirty-seven. They contacted the placing adoption agency, and the agency passed along the news to Nancy's birth mother. Trudy and Chuck told the agency that if the birth mother wanted to call them, they'd be happy to talk with her. Indeed, the birth mother did call, and Trudy said, "We were on the phone for two hours, crying and talking all at the same time." The Clarks made up a scrapbook of pictures and artwork from Nancy's life and sent it to her birth mother. There were more phone calls and a plan to meet even though they lived eight hundred miles apart. As the time of the meeting came closer, Nancy's birth mother wrote, saying she decided not to meet after all.

"I appreciate all you did for Nancy," she wrote. "I know you loved her and were wonderful parents, all that I'd wished for when I gave her up for adoption. Nancy's father turned out to be a terrible person, and I'm glad that Nancy never knew him. My life changed after Nancy's birth. I married a man who also turned out to be not very nice. We are now divorced, and my life has not been easy. I thank you for all the contact and letting me know about Nancy's life and death. Through your sharing of Nancy's life, I know she was happy. That's all I need to know. Meeting you two now would only bring back memories of painful times. I'd rather not do that. I hope you understand. I thank you both from the bottom of my heart."

Nancy's death has been very difficult for the Clarks. After her death, they received numerous letters, poems, and pictures from France from Nancy's friends and coworkers, as well as from the teenagers she helped. Trudy and Chuck knew how wonderful their daughter was, but it was almost overwhelming to them that she was appreciated and loved by so many people—people they didn't know, people who were an ocean away and who were kind enough to want to share their feelings with Nancy's parents.

Meg was thirty-five at the time of her older sister's sudden death, and she had a very difficult time dealing with losing her sister. Meg's sons were in their teens now, and she was close to the time when they would be leaving home. Meg was facing several losses in her life: a sister who had just died and children who were poised to leave the nest.

Meg and her husband decided at that time to become foster parents. A two-year-old was placed with them just about six months after Nancy's death. He was a sickly, difficult child who kept Meg very busy. After a year or so when they had his medical needs under control, Meg and Hank went back for more children. Meg was a wonderful mother and a blessing to several more foster children who found their home with her with the help of Trudy and Chuck, who became surrogate grandparents.

Trudy and Chuck have had many experiences throughout their marriage. They started out as a young, rather inexperienced couple who, throughout their ensuing years, faced many challenges they had never fathomed. They weren't particularly equipped to deal with all that life gave them, but their dedication to each other and to their girls turned them into an amazing family. They have lost their daughter Nancy, but their daughter Meg and her family are filling up their lives, sometimes to a point where it's wonderfully exhausting for them.

There is an amazing closeness now between Meg and her parents. Years ago, Meg and Hank made a point of moving to the same city that Meg had run away from at age sixteen so they could be close to Trudy and Chuck. Meg says she still doesn't understand why her birth mother gave her up for adoption, and she is appalled at her own judgment for leaving her adoptive family to be with Hank at age sixteen. She feels very guilty about that. In later years, Meg told her parents, "I ran away from the wrong family."

If ever there needed to be justification for the existence of the family structure, the Clark family epitomizes it. Trudy and Chuck dealt with a sixteen-year-old who ran off to be with her "true love," and still they were by her side. They lived with an artist personality who was diametrically opposite from their way of life, and they loved her for it. They dealt with the death of a child and survived graciously. We never know how strong we are until we face our challenges. The Clarks are an example of a family who needed to be strong going into the adoption world and emerged even stronger in the end. They faced life situations that their lives had not prepared them for. They are still wonderful salt-of-the-earth-type people, but they can no longer be looked upon as ordinary.

At the end of our interview, we asked, "How has adoption changed your life?"

"It introduced us to circumstances you could never experience unless you adopt," Chuck answered. "If you had only biological children, you'd deal with family that had familiar issues. In adoption, you're exposed to challenges you are not prepared for."

Trudy answered the same question. "It's made us more understanding and very sympathetic to other's problems. We're not critical of others. I tell my friends, 'You can tell me anything.'"

Helen and Vic Jensen, Adoptive Parents

Helen – adoptive mother
Vic – adoptive father
Ken – foster child, later adopted
Ryan – foster child, later adopted
Teresa – foster child, later adopted

Helen and Vic Jensen are not your stereotypical adoptive parents. They are, however, typical of some adoptive parents who, after having biological children, decide to provide a foster home for foster children and then find themselves wanting to adopt some foster children put into their care.

Helen and Vic's daughter was twelve and their son was fourteen when they looked into the possibility of becoming a foster family. They made the stipulation that any foster children had to be younger than their biological children so they would not be in school together. Seven foster children found themselves in the Jensen home over the years, and the Jensens ended up adopting three of them. The others were returned to their biological families or placed in other adoptive homes.

At the time of our interview, their oldest adopted child, Ken, was eighteen years old and in jail for sexually abusing his two younger adopted siblings. The Jensens, obviously, went through some very traumatic times in raising these three foster/adopted children.

Ken had been placed with the Jensens at the age of ten months, but because the birth father had not relinquished his parental rights, Ken's birth father had visitation rights for several years when Ken was of preschool age. It is thought by professionals who later worked with this child that his birth father sexually abused him during these visits. During his childhood, Ken was diagnosed with bipolar disorder, schizophrenia, and attachment disorder. He caused problems in their family from a very early age. He beat their dog with a baseball bat and was a threat to his parents and siblings. He received professional help all throughout his childhood and had a loving, competent family, but Ken, at the age of sixteen, admitted to sexually abusing his younger siblings. He was diagnosed as a psychopath.

The Jensen's second foster/adopted son is mentally handicapped, and Helen says he will always live with them. Ryan, although mentally slow, is mainstreamed in high school and is doing exceptionally well, considering his limitations. The Jensens were told they were given Ryan so he would have a loving place to die. He was not expected to survive, and if he did, this failure-to-thrive baby would never walk or talk. The Jensen's and Ryan proved them all wrong. Ryan has thrived in the Jensen household and has gone way beyond the original limited expectations.

Their third adopted child is a daughter of another race. When the Jensens took Teresa as a foster child, they were told they could not adopt her because they were white and Teresa was black. Over the years, adoption philosophy and laws changed, so they were able to adopt Teresa. Teresa has normal potential and is blossoming within the Jensen home.

The older two (biological) children have been a great help in caring for the younger three (adopted) children. They have been very understanding of the stress that the younger three have put on their parents.

When asked about the original expectations for their foster/adopted children, both parents stated that in looking back, they now realize that they had overly ambitious expectations. Even though they knew the children arrived with innate problems, they felt that with professional help and a loving home, they could overcome these obstacles.

The Jensens said that during this process of raising their last three children, some of their friends drifted away from them. They sensed that these friends didn't want their children playing with the Jensen children. Their own family members were more supportive of their endeavors, being at the very least neutral or somewhat encouraging.

When asked about the birth parents and birth relatives of their children, Helen and Vic said that all three of their adopted children have expressed curiosity and a desire to meet them at some time. "We'd be happy to help our kids find their birth parents," Vic said. "We don't think they'd be a threat to us at all." The Jensens know something of the background of all three birth families and know there are addiction problems and/or mental illness in all of the families.

Both Helen and Vic said adopting their last three children took away some of their personal time together. They said they are now at an age where most of their friends are empty nesters, but they feel their children are keeping them both young. They said their religious faith has been instrumental in keeping their marriage and their family intact throughout their trauma over the years.

At the end of the interview, Vic summed it all up, "I feel good about what we have done with these kids. Ryan would be in an institution now if not with us, and Ken would have been a permanent foster child as both boys were labeled as nonadoptable. I feel our experiences, as difficult as they were, have kept us open-minded and nonjudgmental about life. Others who haven't had our experiences have missed a lot in life. Yes, we'd do it all over again."

Barbara Taylor Blomquist

Carol and Stan Tilton, Adoptive Parents

Carol – adoptive mother
Stan – adoptive father
Charlie – adopted son
Dorothy – adopted daughter

Carol and Stan Tilton stand apart from the other adoptive parents we interviewed. The reason for this was their philosophy toward parenting as well as their religious beliefs. Their two adopted children were twenty-three and twenty-seven at the time of the interview, and even though there were still some ongoing adoption issues, the Tiltons appeared to be the happiest and most fulfilled of all the adoptive parents we spoke with.

Carol had several miscarriages in the beginning years of their marriage. Stan had several adopted cousins and aunts and uncles, so adoption was a very comfortable concept for him to consider. Carol loved children and, in fact, was a teacher. She said initially she was angry at her situation, particularly when she would observe parents mishandle, and even abuse, their children in public places. Carol knew she would be a wonderful mother and felt cheated that her body would not allow her to become one.

The Tiltons had a pleasant experience throughout the adoption process. They liked the agency they worked with, and they liked the adoption worker they had for both children. Their patience was tested, however, by having to wait three years for each of their children. All got off to a good start, and throughout the interview, it seemed that life stayed that way.

During our talk, it became apparent that both were very good parents, and when problems occurred, they were handled as if they were "normal" problems. Their son, Charlie, had a temper and was living in a family where no one else lost his temper. When asked how this was handled, Stan answered that it was handled each and every time, depending on the circumstances. After each temper outburst, Stan was sure to point out to Charlie that losing his temper did not help the situation or problem. This was discussed civilly after all had calmed down. Stan would ask, "Charlie, did losing your temper help your situation? Could you have handled it in a better way, getting a better result?"

Stan stated that there were times (particularly during his children's teenage years) when he was upset with the behavior of his children, but he always caught himself before passing drastic judgment, saying to himself, "You have faults and issues to work on too, but still God loves you unconditionally. How dare you as a father not love your children unconditionally?" Stan said that this thought always calmed him down so that he could deal intelligently with whatever the current problem happened to be and put it all in perspective.

Overall, the Tiltons presented an almost joyous attitude toward their adoption experience. When their children were four and eight, they saw a notice on their church bulletin board asking for foster parents. They both looked at each other in a knowing way and the next morning started on their journey to become foster parents. Over the next ten years, they cared for fifty-six babies who were waiting for adoptive placement. Both Carol and Stan see this wonderful experience as an outcome of their adoption experience. They say they never would have considered becoming foster parents had they not already had the adoption experience to pave their way.

Both parents thought having foster babies in their home was a healthy thing for their children because it showed them the love that adopted children receive all along the way. Their children met birth mothers and adoptive parents during those years.

Many adopted children have a heightened sensitivity to loss. One of the interviewers asked if there were problems with Dorothy and Charlie when the babies left the Tilton home to go to their adoptive homes. Charlie seemed to be affected more by this than his sister, Dorothy, but the Tiltons thought this was a healthy, direct way of explaining the adoption process, experiences of loss being a part of it.

Overall, their parenting experiences seemed positive, and their attitude toward life appeared to have a great part in this. Stan said he would tell his children time and again, "We cannot choose our circumstances, but we can choose our reactions to our circumstances." Problems in the Tilton household were approached as being a part of life, a challenge to work through in order to find success.

Now that their children are in their midtwenties, both parents state that the adoption experience enhanced their lives greatly. They never would have become foster parents, which they thoroughly enjoyed. Carol said their home seemed much calmer during the times when they had a foster baby there. Both expressed that because of their adoption experience, over the years they have become more insightful, more open-minded, and more devout in their religion. Carol and Stan both said they clearly now see a divine plan for their lives, and they feel very blessed and pleased with the plan.

There was a significant difference in the demeanor and attitude of the Tilton's and other adoptive parents. All the parents interviewed said that even though they went through some difficult times, they treasured the experience because of how living life with adoption changed them. They would not want to go back to being the limited people they were before. The obvious difference with the Tilton's was their attitude that everyone has problems and that's what life is about, solving and overcoming problems. They did not attribute their problems to an unfair world but accepted them as life itself.

Carol and Stan said they always looked upon their two children as gifts who arrived in their home with gifts of their own. They never tried to mold their children into something they were not. They accepted and respected the uniqueness of each child. Stan told his son many times he had the best of both worlds: Charlie's inherited athletic and scholastic prowess, both of which outpaced his own, along with the love and appreciation of his adoptive parents. The Tilton's stated a great admiration for their two children and the unique people that they are. They feel fortunate to be their parents.

There was no hint of disappointment or complaining about the hard times, only gratitude for being able to parent two wonderful human beings, flaws and all.

Their obvious joy with their life came through with their great sense of shared accomplishment. They stated that they felt they were living out God's will, and this has to be a good thing. They said they didn't understand it at the beginning, but as life unfolded, they saw what their destined contribution to life was to become. Their positive attitudes meshed with each other, and they presented themselves as a strong team working toward a common goal of loving and raising healthy, happy children: their own two, plus giving fifty-six babies waiting to be adopted a loving home in which to start their life's journey.

Mary and Craig Wheeler, Adoptive Parents

Mary – adoptive mother
Craig – adoptive father
Todd – grandson, adopted son

Mary and Craig are the adoptive parents that all adoption social workers hope for. Mary was a social worker herself before they adopted a biological brother and sister, who were ages eight and nine at the time of their adoption. They were told that the children were so damaged by birth parents and foster and failed adoptive homes that the children would be better off institutionalized because they were not a good potential for a successful adoption.

Mary and Craig went through with the adoption with very few expectations of having a perfect family. Their eyes were opened to the facts of what their lives could become dealing with the aftereffects that abuse imposed on their young children, but they also were young and hopeful they could make a difference in the lives of these two children.

After the usual "honeymoon" period of dealing with smiling, obedient children, reality settled in, and they had to deal with the abuse issues and their aftermath. When we interviewed Mary and Craig, their children were thirty-six and thirty-seven. Mary and Craig had spent years dealing with low achievement, drug and alcohol abuse, jail time, lying, stealing, and promiscuity. As young adults, both their children engaged in behavior that resulted in abortions as well as live births. Neither child finished high school. Both children left their home prematurely. Their son left at fifteen to go into a series of residential treatment centers, and their daughter left at sixteen, when she became pregnant.

Now that the children are in their midthirties, Mary and Craig don't have regular contact with them. They haven't seen either one in four years. Both children are living with significant others (after several failed marriages) and have steady jobs. Mary religiously sends cards to them at Christmastime, Valentine's Day, Easter, birthdays, and Halloween. She lets them know their door is always open. Both Mary and Craig are hoping that as the children mature into their forties, they will become solid citizens and they can become a true family. This has been their hope all along.

Their daughter gave birth to a son when she was seventeen years old, and as time passed, it became obvious to all that she was not equipped to care for her baby. When Todd was six years old, Mary and Craig offered to adopt him so he could have a stable homelife. Their daughter agreed, as she realized she was not doing a good job. Todd, now seventeen, knows of his mother's shortcomings although she is becoming more stable now. He has loving grandparents, whom he calls Mom and Dad, and has faint hope that his birth mother will become responsible someday and reenter his life. She has been invited to various events in his life—like ball games, graduations, etc.—but has yet to appear. Todd has little hope that she will ever reappear in his life, but Mary and Craig still have hope that she will.

For more than twenty years, Mary's and Craig's lives have been stressful—filled with police encounters, their children being expelled from multiple schools as well as residential treatment centers, and sleepless nights wondering where their children were. When asked in the interview if they were sorry they had taken on such a difficult task as raising these two children, there was no hesitation. Almost in unison, they said, "Oh, of course not."

Craig went on to say, "Look, these kids were going to be institutionalized or in foster care forever. Can you imagine where they would be now? At least now they are on the right side of the law, in relatively stable relationships, and are gainfully employed. We still hope that all the good we've done for them pays off. We know they are better off in life because we adopted them. When we first laid eyes on them, we knew they were our kids. We knew we'd stick by them no matter what. Always. We hope that one day they will walk through our open door. Then we will have our family back."

Craig and Mary epitomize many adoptive parents who spend years and years attempting to heal the wounds that other adults have inflicted upon their children. Craig's and Mary's children had been in seven foster and adoptive homes before being adopted by them. Two of those homes were failed adoptions. By the ages of eight and nine, these children had been abused and didn't have a very positive view of themselves or their world. They spent many years in counseling and had loving parents by their side, but still, today as adults, they are struggling with issues of trust, loss, and grief.

Mary laughs when she says they can't win with their relatives. Half of them think they parent too permissively, and the other half thinks they parent too strictly. The general public, which is not aware of the results of child neglect or abuse, often look to the parents as being the culprits when children misbehave. Fortunately, Mary and Craig have a sense of humor about it because they know they don't have the time to educate people about all the issues their children are facing. They've been too busy trying to undo other adults' wrongs.

Kathy and Bill Wright, Adoptive Parents

Kathy – adoptive mother
Bill – adoptive father
Danielle – adopted daughter

The Wright family is an example of faith and patience, particularly on the part of Kathy. One of the Wright's adopted daughters left home when she was fifteen and didn't return for twenty years.

There was contact only four times during that twenty-year period. For years, Kathy and Bill didn't know where their daughter was or what she was doing, or even if she was still alive. The four phone calls they did receive from Danielle during that time all ended with Kathy telling Danielle she hoped she would come home, and saying they would pay for a plane ticket for her to fly home from wherever she was.

The Wrights adopted two sons and two daughters during the 1970s. For the most part, Kathy said their life was fairly normal, but Danielle, their second child, harbored a lot of anger, which came out in temper tantrums as a toddler and viciousness as she grew older. The source of this anger was a mystery to the family. The other children didn't exhibit this behavior, and unfortunately, they were often the victims of Danielle's bad moods. Many occasions, vacations, and times together as a family were spoiled by Danielle's hostility toward other family members.

Kathy said she wasn't sure how to handle this anger since she couldn't understand its source. Everyone else in the family was happy and productive, and there were many times Danielle was sweet as well. She seemed overly sensitive, and Kathy said she found herself filtering almost everything she said to Danielle in hopes of avoiding a resentful or angry response.

During Danielle's sophomore year in high school, she started taking marijuana, and her behavior spiraled downhill rapidly. She skipped school, stole money from family members, and was away from her family more than before, spending time with her new friends.

The summer Danielle turned fifteen, Kathy and Bill were at the end of their rope, not knowing how to help Danielle, and there was very little help available for families experiencing what they were. Kathy said she spent days making phone calls and getting a lot of sympathy from people who said they couldn't help her. They commiserated with her, saying they got a lot of phone calls like hers but didn't know anywhere she could go for answers.

Kathy and Bill thought that perhaps sending their daughter away to summer camp might help. It would certainly relieve the family of the dysfunction Danielle was causing and give them all some peace. Danielle thought this was a great idea since she could get away from her family where she didn't feel she was appreciated.

Near the end of the summer, Danielle called and told her parents she wasn't coming home. She said she liked Arizona and wanted to live there permanently. She said she'd go to school and get a job to support herself, and she would no longer be a part of their family.

Kathy and Bill were shocked and felt helpless. Bill flew out to Arizona to intercede and bring Danielle home, but she had already left camp, and no one knew where she'd gone. She had packed her things and left during the night, three days before the end of camp.

Bill didn't know what to do. He said he hardly knew where to start, so he called and visited some agencies that were in the business of providing for runaways who needed food or clothing. The police were also notified, but there was no word of Danielle.

After a few days in Arizona, Bill flew home to a distraught Kathy. Days turned into weeks and weeks into months. The first few months after Danielle disappeared, Kathy said that her heart raced every time the phone rang. Then her thinking changed, and she realized the news could be good or it could be bad. As it turned out, none of the phone calls were from Danielle or about Danielle.

Their other three children still needed parents, and Kathy and Bill doubled down on their parenting activities. Kathy increased her volunteering at their children's schools just so she wouldn't be home alone with time to think. When driving, she'd often see a teenager who resembled Danielle, and it always startled her. Her sadness would overcome her and start her tears flowing again.

Kathy said she had to keep thinking of the good she knew was inside of Danielle. Much of it was covered up with anger, but deep down, Danielle was a sensitive and sweet girl. Kathy concentrated on the happy memories where Danielle would help her younger siblings or bring home a stray animal, no matter what kind. When Danielle was six years old, she brought home baby birds that she'd taken from a nest, thinking they must be hungry. Kathy couldn't bring herself to imagine where Danielle was or what she was doing to survive. Bill and Kathy were a strong support for each other, but Bill left every morning to go to work. He had a place where his mind could concentrate on other aspects of life. Kathy didn't have that.

The first of four phone calls came at 11:30 p.m. one Thanksgiving night two years after Danielle left them. Kathy had extended family for dinner, and she struggled during the day to keep her composure so she wouldn't break down and cry. The family wasn't complete without her lost daughter, but she was pleased she survived the day without showing her sadness. The late-night phone call was from Danielle. During the call, Kathy urged her daughter to come home, but Danielle told her mother that she was fine and not to worry about her. Danielle wouldn't tell Kathy where she was but did end the conversation with "I love you, Mom." After they hung up, all the tears that were choked back during Thanksgiving Day poured out from Kathy.

Kathy said it's hard to believe, but life went on after that. She said that had someone told her that one of her children would leave home for twenty years, she couldn't have handled the thought. But she said she had no choice but to continue being a mother and a wife, albeit a continually sad one.

Kathy started writing letters to her daughter, knowing her daughter would never read them. She was so honest in releasing her emotions in these letters that she hid them so no one would come across them. At the beginning, it was a way for her to express her fear about Danielle's welfare. In time, it was an avenue for Kathy to safely vent her resentment for what her daughter had done to the family, and eventually, it was a way for Kathy to express her love for her daughter. No one will ever see these letters, and Kathy said she probably will burn them one day. During all those years, it was a way to connect with her absent daughter. She felt she was connecting with Danielle while writing, and that felt good. Kathy said she always had to be careful at the end that her tears didn't fall onto the page and smudge the print.

Throughout the next twenty years, there were three more phone calls, which were as vague as the first one Kathy received on that Thanksgiving night. They knew Danielle was still alive, but that's about all they knew about her.

Kathy started to search in bookstores and libraries for answers to Danielle's behavior. There wasn't much available at the time to help Kathy, but she absorbed all she could. She learned that some adoptees held repressed anger about being "given away," often not realizing that was the source of their deeply recessed anger. They could not accept love from anyone because they thought they were unlovable. They were unlovable because they had been given away. Their underlying anger comes from this hostile feeling toward their adoption and everyone involved in it. This was one answer Kathy found, and she thought it was the right answer for Danielle's behavior.

Kathy's religion provided her some comfort, along with the thought that one day Danielle would return to them. Kathy vowed that when that day came, she would welcome Danielle with joy and unconditional love. Kathy said she had many years to deal with her anger and resentment toward Danielle. After years of feeling responsible for the whole situation, Kathy said she found her balance by thinking Danielle had made this decision by herself. Kathy, naturally, had done some second-guessing about what she as a mother may have done wrong to drive her daughter away. Then the thought would come to her that her other three children are happy and normal, so maybe it wasn't all her fault, after all.

Kathy said it was at this point that her anger and resentment toward Danielle fell away and was replaced with pity, sympathy, and a hope that her daughter would one day realize how much she had been loved. Kathy said she stubbornly hung on to this attitude and, by doing so, was able to live out her life somewhat free from the overwhelming sadness that had gripped her in the earlier years.

The separation ended twenty years after it started when Danielle called her father at work and asked if she could come home to surprise her mother on her mother's birthday. Bill knew this would be a shock for Kathy, so he told Kathy about Danielle's coming home. Both parents had apprehension, as well as relief and joy, about the impending occasion. They didn't know what to expect. There was a part of them that was afraid of what they would see.

Only Bill and Kathy met Danielle's plane. The other three children were grown and married by this time, and two of them lived in another state. Kathy said her hands turned ice-cold as they waited for their daughter to come off the plane. When they finally did see her, even though they knew she was now thirty-five years old, Kathy said she was still shocked, and it hit her how much of Danielle's life they had not been a part of. Danielle looked healthy and happy as she approached them. She was smiling but seemed hesitant about how she would be received.

Kathy said she knew at that instant that she had to set the stage for the rest of their lives. She rushed toward Danielle, embracing her for a long time. Bill said he hugged his daughter as well, but it was hard for him not to feel some resentment toward her.

At the time of our interview with the Wrights, Danielle had been back in the family for a little over five years, or, as Kathy stated with a smile, "five years, two months, and three weeks."

Kathy said those five years have been like a Walt Disney movie. Danielle's guilt and remorse at what she put her family through have been a heavy burden for her. Kathy has tried to help her daughter overcome this burden by encouraging her to concentrate on the present and the future. Throughout Danielle's twenty-year absence, several of Kathy's friends had had a falling out with their children. Kathy saw these women turn into bitter, revengeful mothers, vowing they would never forgive the pain their children had put them through, or were still putting them through.

Kathy vowed she would never let herself become so bitter, although it would be easy to do. Instead, she realized that Danielle was doing the best she could even though it was pitifully lacking. Kathy felt that one day Danielle would return to the family, and when that day came, she wanted to be filled with love, not hate, for her daughter. Kathy knew also, from a selfish point of view, that she was happier than her counterparts who went the bitter route. After Danielle returned, two of Kathy's friends who had not reconciled with their children dropped Kathy as a friend. Kathy was happy now, and they were not. They no longer had a lost child as a common element.

As it turns out, Danielle had gotten her GED while she was gone, and also took some business courses at a community college. She had fared fairly well in supporting herself.

There hasn't been a lot of deep conversation as to just where Danielle was and what she was doing during those twenty years, but Kathy said she actually didn't care to know. She wanted a clean start and thought that if she knew the particulars of her daughter's life during that time, Kathy might be tempted to judge her, and Kathy didn't want to do that. She had missed so much of their life together; she was just grateful they were together again. Kathy said she and Danielle both have made an effort to realize that Danielle was doing the best she could at the time with trying to deal with her feelings. No one knew really what the cause of the problem was at the time. Back then loss issues were not recognized as an aftermath of adoption.

Kathy said that eventually Danielle may tell them more about those missed years, and when that time came, it would be the right time for Danielle. Danielle did announce that she'd been drug-free for four years prior to returning home. Kathy was gratified to see her daughter's new image. She showed no anger and seemed unusually patient. She has become a delightful, caring woman, showing great appreciation and compassion for all the family. Danielle seems eager to be back in the family fold again.

Kathy tells of one conversation she and Danielle had. It was a pleasant conversation, and Kathy says she can't remember what they were talking about, but while she was talking, Danielle interrupted and blurted out in a surprised voice, "There was love here all the time. I just couldn't see it. I was too angry." The women just looked at each other. Danielle was as startled as Kathy at the statement she'd just made. A long hug and a few tears followed.

Shortly after her return home, Danielle found a job and an apartment about twenty miles from her parents, and they continue to have a loving, respectful relationship. She has a job she is happy with, and she continues to make new friends. Danielle is very attentive to her parents now, perhaps making up for lost time. She makes a great effort to be with them as much as possible and calls often, with the phone calls lasting an hour or more. She appears to have a great appreciation for the people she now sees them to be. She is grateful they love her, and now that she is mature and self-assured, she can accept their love and return it to them.

When all the children were young, Danielle's siblings had a hard time dealing with her disruptive behavior. Now that they are all adults, they understand that Danielle had problems as a child that she was not able to cope with successfully, and since no one understood them, there was no help. Kathy is so thankful that they are a unified family once again and feels badly that she didn't understand the loss and feeling of isolation that caused Danielle's disruptive behavior. Each time they are all together, the family feelings are getting closer and warmer. Kathy and Bill both are so grateful they are a full family once again. The past is past, and they love the present.

Love doesn't solve all of adoption's problems, but in a case like this, love can help to bring a lost child home again.

The Riders, Adoptive Family

This story came from the oldest biological daughter of a family that was a mixed family in several aspects. When we heard her story, she had children and grandchildren, so she could look back at her childhood with a deep perspective. Adoption is usually thought of just affecting the adopted child and the adoptive parents in the aftermath of placing a child in a family. This story shows a serious impact on the whole family.

It particularly shows that many, if not most, parents who are raising biological children can have a hard time raising adopted children who arrive in their home damaged from either a bad environment they have been removed from or from multiple placements before arriving in their adoptive home. These children often have special needs that the normal population of parents is not prepared to handle.

Attachment disorder is a common issue that accompanies many older children into a new home. They have given up trying to bond, knowing they will undoubtedly be moving on, anyway. Stability has not been in their experience, so they feel the need to look out only for themselves. They know from experience that adults have left them before and think adults will undoubtedly be leaving them again. No need to bond. They'll only be hurt once again.

In the Rider family, the first five children were biological: four daughters and then a son. The mother in the family didn't have a good relationship with her own mother but was close to her maternal grandmother, who had five biological children and then took in five of her nieces and nephews after they were orphaned. Mrs. Rider was inspired by her grandmother and idolized what her grandmother had done with her life.

When the Riders' biological children ranged from age seven to eighteen, Mrs. Rider decided she wanted to adopt children. Seven-year-old twin boys were placed in their family. They had been in eleven foster homes in their short lives and arrived with many problems, mostly caused by their birth mother drinking while pregnant, which caused fetal alcohol syndrome in her sons. One boy was legally blind. Like some other twins, the two boys talked "twin talk," their own language that only they could understand.

The family pediatrician advised the Riders against this adoption, but with only one son in the family, the parents thought bringing the twins into the family would be company for their sole son. It actually took time and nurturing away from him, and as a young child, he thought he wasn't a good-enough son and that was why his parents adopted more boys.

Much time and energy had to be given to these two little boys, which took nurturing energy away from the biological children. Mrs. Rider, in modern times, would probably be diagnosed as depressed, which caused her to sleep every afternoon. She obviously went into the adoption thinking she could mother these two little boys. Like so many adoptive parents, she was not prepared to handle their special needs. After the adoption, the Riders did seek professional help, but it was of little help. The older children were pretty much on their own, at times helping with the younger twins but not getting the mothering they needed.

They tell a story that describes the dysfunction in their family at this time. One of the younger biological girls, about nine at the time, would disappear every day during the summer, walking a mile down the road to spend the day with a family who had a small farm. During the summer, she spent all day there, especially loving working with the horses. She wasn't particularly missed at home. She'd be back home for dinner but never told anyone in her family where she'd been. That was her escape from the dysfunction, and she didn't want any one family member to know, fearing they would spoil her good times. She later said those were the happiest times of her childhood.

The two older girls, who were sixteen and eighteen when the twins arrived, went on to have happy, productive lives. The younger three biological children struggled. Drugs and divorces were part of their later experiences. Even as adults, the younger siblings still resent the two older girls. The younger three blame their two older sisters for not sensing the situation as it was and helping to nurture them when their mother didn't, even though the older girls were teens at the time and also in need of nurturing and support. The older girls (now women) have tried to have family reunions now that they are all adults with grandchildren, but the anger and resentment still expressed by their younger siblings ruins every gathering. The younger three have had troubled lives, including bad marriages and divorces.

When the twins arrived in the Rider family, they brought disruptive behavior with them. There were run-ins with the law, and at age fifteen, they ran away to another state. Their adoptive father followed them to bring them back home, but Mrs. Rider said she couldn't handle them anymore, and the boys were institutionalized until they were eighteen.

At age eighteen, the boys both went to the East Coast but not together. There was no contact with the Rider family, and a few years later, when some family members tried to find them, they were unsuccessful.

About twenty years later, they did have success in contacting them. The Riders learned that one twin had been heavily into drugs and had been homeless for some time. He was killed by other drug addicts who beat him to death to steal his drugs. The surviving twin moved backed to their home city, and the two older sisters welcomed him and helped him get settled. After a very short time, they realized that their adopted brother was taking over their lives, making daily demands on their time and trying to make them feel guilty when they couldn't help him. The renewed relationship—

which involved including him for holidays, dinners, family events, etc.—had to end when the sisters realized he was sapping most of their energy with his needs.

The difference in the five biological siblings is interesting, the first two having had enough nurturing to continue on with their lives while the younger three never were given the emotional foundation they needed. The mother's depression was a factor in her ability to nurture, and when the needy twins arrived, she was overwhelmed by demands she couldn't handle. Today there are experts in adoption issues that help situations like this that will help the whole family deal with special needs, but the Riders adopted before this specialized help was available. Adopting the twins affected every member in the family, and still does to this day.

The five siblings are not close in adulthood because of the retained resentment of the younger three against the older two. The older two have reached out to help their younger siblings, giving them financial and emotional support, but this has just caused a wider divide, making the younger ones feel more inadequate.

The father in this family was a very successful businessman, and from an outsider's point of view, they appeared to be a happy family. They had dinner every night together, the proverbial test for a well-functioning family, but there was a lack of nurturing from their mother once the twins arrived. She was overwhelmed by their needs. Even though she probably was clinically depressed, she might have been able to meet the needs for all her biological children had she not been overwhelmed by the twins.

Years ago, when relinquishment and abandonment issues were not given their due, there was little or inadequate outside professional help in situations like this. Babies and children were placed into adoptive homes, and adoption agencies didn't recognize that many of these children would need special help that adoptive parents, or any parent, would not recognize or know how to handle.

Now, fortunately, there is recognition of this fact, and support is available. Adoption issues are special, and it takes an adoption specialist to work with adoptive families with troubled children. Those in the adoption field recommend strongly that if a family goes into a situation like this, they will need adoption counseling—not help from just any professional but only from an adoption specialist who understands the depths of loss and adoption issues. There are also excellent books available now that go to the core of the loss issue that some adoptees face. The important thing is to deal with the source of behavior, not only the behavior itself, which is merely a symptom of the turmoil underneath.

As this story shows, family members can be affected by adoption problems caused by children with abandonment and multiple-placement issues. Many parents think love will solve their issues. It will help, but a deep understanding of the cause of adopted children's problems is a must. A deep, extended study of adoption issues or engaging an adoption expert who truly understands adoption cause-and-effect behavior are the paths needed for success. Unfortunately, too many years have passed before the adoption world recognized this, and too many people suffered because of it.

SECTION V

13

Loss and Gain

Those who have lived long enough to experience some ups and downs in their lives know that one can usually find a silver lining in many things that life puts in our path. Adoption is no exception.

In talking with the interviewees, it was obvious that many of them built their character and their lives on the challenges that adoption provided. Many said they would not undo a thing from their past. Their lows were low indeed, but their highs were exalting. In overcoming what they faced (and weren't prepared to face), they said they turned into a far better person than they had been before. They would not ever want to go back to the person they were before. Their intensity and insight and appreciation for life were heightened by being forced to go deep within themselves to find the love and compassion they never knew was there. Many now spoke positively about their journey although in the midst of their challenges, it would not have been so. There was a joy to their expression when they said they feel fortunate to now see life through their new perspective.

During the interview process, the person being interviewed showed their attitude within a few minutes. Some were stuck at the beginning phase of their involvement in adoption and were resentful and angry, while others had moved beyond that and were grateful for how the adoption process had developed them into a better person than they feel they might have been otherwise. Both adoptive parents and adoptees expressed this.

All people involved in the adoption experience can feel both loss and gain. It's safe to say that for most involved, the gains, by far, outweigh the losses. First the losses will be looked at, and later, the gains that often originated from these losses will be discussed.

People who understand adoption widely acknowledge that all three sides of the adoption triad experience loss. It is accepted that adoption is based on loss. The adoptee loses his birth family, the birth parents lose their child, and the adoptive family has already lost their (potential) birth family even before they adopt. This is much too simple. There are many, many ramifications to all these losses, which will be discussed in this section. The real discussion of loss needs to include the result of that loss and any gains caused by the loss.

In our interviews, people seemed very aware of how their lives had changed because of their adoption experience. In most cases, the impact was perhaps the one most powerful aspect in their life. However, they often looked at their life as a whole and not just at the result of any adoption loss. In other words, they presented a perspective of their lives, which included the aftermath and results of the original loss. They were very aware of the path their life took *after* the adoption process. They looked at the whole picture.

We will discuss all three sides of the triad but start with the adoptee first since he appears to be in the middle of the adoption experience.

14

Adoptee Loss and Gain

Here is a list of the adoptee's losses:

- Loss of his birth parents, aunts, uncles, grandparents, cousins, and potential siblings
- Loss of his heritage, traditions, and culture
- Loss of personal knowledge about himself and inherited traits
- Loss of his true identity, not being linked genetically to anyone he knows
- Loss of "belonging" to a family by natural biological right
- Loss of sense of security within his family; some harbor the thought "I was given away once, so it can always happen again"

There are implications to all these stated losses. Their sense of identity and a sense of belonging—these are the losses that seem to make the most impact on adoptees. This is what they talk about the most and say they miss the most.

It is extremely rare to hear an adoptee say (when given the hypothetical choice) that in hindsight, he would have preferred to be raised by his birth parents. From an adult point of view, the adoptee can see that his birth family often presented an unhealthy environment. He can see that his adoptive family almost always provided more stability and opportunities to view life from a healthy perspective. Even when the adoptee had complaints about his adoptive family and his experience was not the best, he still said he thought he was better off with his adoptive family rather than his birth family. He still felt a sense of loss, however. Intellectually, he knows it was the right decision all around, but there often is a sadness that the decision had to be made at all.

One forty-five-year-old adoptee was an exception to this finding. He had a relatively good childhood and stated that his adoptive parents loved him. His sense (or lack of sense) of identity was so strong that he said he wished he would have been raised by his birth family. He smiled and went on to say, "Of course, I'd probably be in prison by now because my birth father died in prison and two of my brothers are there now, but at least I'd know who I am."

He had been struggling with his identity issue for many years and was pleased when he found his birth family, but it confused him even more as to his identity. His adoptive family was from a small town where minorities were rare, and he was raised to be prejudicial. When he found out through his search that he had some minority blood in his heritage, he had to absorb this into his new identity. His adoptive family was on the right side of the law, and some members of his birth family were on the wrong side of the law. This and other issues caused some conflict he had to face.

His struggle for identity was so unsuccessful during the forty-five years before he searched that he was ecstatic when he finally found his birth family. They lived in a nearby town, and he was able to contact some of them, but some birth family members did not want to meet him, and he was drawn into the dynamics of a large dysfunctional family. This scene was new to him, having had no similar experience, and there were times when he regretted that his search in finding his birth family members was successful. He did say that finding his identity was satisfying, and this appeared to be valuable to him in spite of the fact that it was accompanied by newly complicated family relationships.

In some instances, a sense of not belonging appears to be the foundation of an adoptee's identity. He feels strongly that because he is different from other family members, he is not in the right place. This is not a universal feeling among adoptees, of course, but it seems to be rather common among those who search for their birth families. Some biological children and adults often feel that they are different from their biological families, that they just don't belong, they aren't understood by their families. The adoptee has the trump card in this situation, however, because of his removal from any genetically related person.

Realizing they do not share genetic material with their adoptive parents, some adoptees feel the need to forge their own identity. Sometimes there is some biological information available but often little or none. This gives them the freedom to look at life without any legacy. This can provide a sense of loss or an impetus to explore freely. They experiment with experiences until they find their comfort zone and can proceed to develop themselves into the image they want. They appear to be very confident because they are truly themselves. They had fewer boundaries than biological children, so the whole world and its opportunities were open to them. Because they felt no preconceived constraints, they were able to develop in a way that pleased them.

On the other hand, adoptees who were motivated by mourning for their birth legacies had a hard time. The fact that their birth families could not care for them seemed to be the one profound legacy that created their self-image. This appeared to be their identity, period. They felt unwanted and unloved by their birth families, and often wondered if the whole world looked at them this way. This is a heavy burden.

Because of this possible effect on any adopted child, adoptive parents need to constantly reinforce the philosophy that we all are what we make of ourselves. Whether adopted or not, people are responsible for who they are and who they become.

At times, an adoptee can shed his negative image by himself. Often, it is done with therapy, but sometimes, the adoptee just becomes tired of being the victim and eventually sees himself as a person, not an adoptee. Nick is an example of this. He sounded very much like a victim during our interview. He said that during his whole life, he sought out people who were unhealthy for him. He had a bad marriage because he chose a girl he didn't really like but thought he deserved. He sounded like an adolescent boy who wondered who he was and where he was headed. Both of Nick's birth parents as well as his adoptive parents either attended college or graduated from college, but Nick's self-esteem was so low that he didn't think he was good enough to attempt college.

A short time after our interview, Nick found his birth mother. After a few years of getting to know his wonderful new birth family, he found that he was no happier than before. He stated, "I don't fit in there, either." With this revelation, something finally clicked within Nick; perhaps he was tired of beating himself up. A short time after this, Nick announced he had met a wonderful woman. He married her and had a baby on the way, and very importantly, he was happy with himself.

Nick now had a sense of who he was, and it wasn't dependent on either his adoptive family or his birth family. He had found himself. He had thought for years that his identity secret lay within his birth family but found out after his reunion with them that his identity secret was within himself all along. He now experienced a sense of belonging that had eluded him his whole life. He knew he belonged to his wife, his adoptive family, his birth family, and himself. Others embraced him all along, but he wasn't able to accept their love until he could accept himself. Nick is now complete, a very happy man.

The adoptee does not live his life with his birth family. This loss can be fantasized about for years. A child will often glamorize what his life would be like if he were still with his birth family, and the true facts that emerge after a search can be a bit of a reality shock. Lisa, who was one of five adopted daughters, said she and her sisters used to sit around and make up wonderful stories about their birth families. One sister had dark eyes and dark hair, so she fantasized she was the daughter of a Spanish princess. Another sister was very proper, so she must be the daughter of a lord and lady from England. Their stories were always positive, and even though the young girls undoubtedly knew they were romantic fantasies, their stories provided a positive spin on their birth identity. The difference is they acknowledged all along that they were fairy tales.

Lisa attended an adoption support group and heard adoptive parents say that their adoption workers instructed them to tell their children the truth about their birth parents, including drug addiction, a negative lifestyle, etc. Lisa was shocked to hear this and jumped in to refute this philosophy. "Oh no, your child has to think he comes from something good," she said. "After all, that is part of his identity. You don't want to fill him with a negative image of himself!"

Many families, particularly those who adopt from foreign countries or transracially, now incorporate customs and traditions from the culture of their adopted child. This is healthy and adds to the child's identity, adding positive factors and providing a base to build on.

All of the losses the adoptee has to incorporate into his life affect his sense of identity. A person's sense of belonging affects his sense of identity. Some adoptees say they not only feel they don't belong to their family but also have a hard time feeling they belong anywhere. In these cases, their identity image is so muddled that they say they always feel different from others. This is their concept, an internal issue that in previous years adoptive parents were not made aware of. Adoptive parents assumed, because they knew their adopted children belonged to them, that their children would also feel they belonged to their adoptive family. Now we are hearing that some adoptees never shared this feeling.

These interviews demonstrated over and over that if adoptive families had only one thing to concentrate on, it would be to cement their adoptive child into their family so that he knew, without a doubt, that he belonged and was in the right place. Don't take it for granted that a child feels secure. Adopted children need this fact reinforced over and over throughout their childhood. Adoptees told us this was a crucial piece to their puzzle of self-realization.

Here is a list of the adoptee's gains:

- Usually placed in a two-parent home in comparison to the prospect of being raised by a single mother
- Usually adopted by a family in a higher socioeconomic position, which could provide a higher education and other advantages
- In their teen years, adoptees often realize they are not fettered by unknown biological family limitations nor by adoptive family expectations since they are not genetically attached to their adoptive family.
- Has the knowledge that he was truly a wanted child and enjoys a high-appreciation status
- Adopted adults often state that their being adopted made them a deeper and stronger person because of their introspective effort to resolve their identity issues.

In looking at the list above, it's undoubtedly safe to say that adopted children have issues that a biological child does not experience. A sense of belonging is basic to the human experience, and coming to terms with "Where do I belong?" can be critical in growing up, whether one is adopted or not.

Adult adoptees who have successfully resolved this issue say emphatically that being adopted and working through their identity issues developed them into a finer person than they might have been otherwise. They express that they have more empathy and are more introspective because of living in a family that is genetically different than they are. There is no automatic tie provided by nature, so the bonding had to be a conscious issue. It becomes an intellectual and consistent effort and is not taken for granted. On a grander scale, it exhibits humanity at its finest. This involves compassion, tolerance, and thoughtfulness at a deep level.

Adoptees are often found to have a higher IQ when compared to their birth siblings who were kept in their birth family. Parental attitude toward education and educational opportunities are generally given more emphasis in adoptive families.

The task of all teenagers is to develop into responsible adults. These years are often difficult for the teens, as well as the parents, as teens assert independence and look at the world through their own eyes and not their parents' eyes. A lot of this is trial and error, as many parents who have lived through this know. A biological child innately knows he belongs by birth, by nature, by definition to his biological parents and hence his biological family. An adopted child may not feel this inevitable tie as defined by nature. His moving away from his family to venture out into the world can be scarier if he feels his adoptive family is a man-made family and does not come with a guarantee of belonging. The teenage years can be a much more volatile time for an adopted child. He's worked for years to gain a sense of belonging to people he's not biologically related to, and now the world is telling him he must become independent.

Adoptees have expressed this dilemma: they want to hang on to their family they've worked hard to embrace, but their friends are trying to spread their wings and move away from their families. Will the adopted child still be part of his family if he becomes independent?

In some families, this is more of an issue than in others. If the tie is tight, it is easier for the adopted child to develop into what's in his natural and genetic makeup. Many adoptees in their adult years say they loved the freedom of exploring avenues outside of the family limits. They felt secure in their placement and felt they had the backing and blessing of their family to try many new things, even though they might be very different from their adoptive family's world. They say they felt a true freedom to just be themselves. They felt no expectations or limitations from either their biological family or their adoptive family. They felt this was an advantage their adopted status brought them.

Young people who could successfully go this route had been encouraged to develop a strong sense of their own individual identity as a human being, knowing they were unconditionally supported and loved by their adoptive family.

15

Birth-Parent Loss and Gain

The birth parents' losses are the following:

- Loss of knowing their child as an extension of themselves
- Possible loss of a potential relationship or marriage with the other birth parent
- Guilt and loss of some self-esteem, knowing they "gave away their own baby"
- Loss of trust in relationships (if the birth mother was deserted by the birth father)
- Loss of openness, honesty; living with a "secret," sometimes not even told to their eventual spouse and subsequent children
- If a teenager, the loss of a part of their childhood

People don't always consider that there are two birth parents. It is usually the birth mother who is concentrated on when it comes to discussing the relinquishment of a baby. We talked with birth fathers who, thirty or forty years after the birth of their child, still longed to see their child. Some birth fathers realize in adulthood how traumatic it must have been for the birth mother to have been abandoned by them. They feel guilt about this now and carry it sadly.

In the interviews, we asked the question "In hindsight, knowing what you know now, do you wish you had kept your child?" Virtually all of the birth parents stated that they had no choice back then and realize now that they are older adults, the decision to place their child into an adoptive family was the best, the healthiest decision they could make. They say perhaps they could have dropped out of school and taken a job, given their baby to various relatives to babysit but realize that was not the best for their child. The trauma of giving up their child does not go away with the years, however. Birth parents still shed tears when talking about the child they relinquished even though that child was well into adulthood now.

Birth mothers, in particular, appeared to have ongoing issues after relinquishing their babies. Some felt angry at their own parents who made that decision for them. Up until the last few decades, it was considered the only proper decision to make. Unwed mothers were not expected to raise a baby single-handedly, nor was that practice accepted by society at the time. A lingering anger against their parents was still carried by some birth parents. At the time of their baby's birth, often the birth mother's shame and guilt took over her life. It wasn't until years later when that mellowed a little that they then felt free to be angry at their own parents, the people responsible for the loss of their baby.

Most birth mothers who have not been reunited with their birth children said they just want to make sure their children are happy and have good lives. Birth mothers traditionally say they don't want to intrude or complicate their children's lives by intruding on them. However, many do go on to say that if their child wants a relationship with them, they would be overwhelmed with joy. After their indoctrination in a home for unwed mothers, there is still a part of them that feels they do not have any right to their biological child.

We found in our interviews that if the birth mother sought and found her child, she would say, "I wish he had searched for me." Conversely, if the birth child searched and found his birth mother, he would say, "I wish she had searched for me." These statements were expressed sadly and wistfully. They all wanted to be sought after, not the one doing the seeking.

When contacted by their birth children, some birth mothers deny that they had ever given birth to them. Sometimes their current husband knows of the birth, but their subsequent children do not. Birth parents often find it hard to expose this facet of their life to their later children who were born into their current family. However, if they proceed with a search and/or reunion, birth parents are pleasantly surprised and relieved at the casualness with which the information is received by family members. Many of their subsequent children go on a dedicated search to locate their half-sibling, and this search is often more vigorous than that of the birth parent's. The feeling of ownership of the relationship with a half-sibling appears to have no guilt attached, whereas the birth parent often wonders if the relinquished person may harbor resentment at being given up. This fear is a very strong motivator for the birth parent not to search, but they hope that instead their child finds them.

Many birth mothers don't have lingering anger or resentment toward the birth father. At the time, they felt betrayed by them if the pregnancy ended their relationship, but now that these women are adults, they realize that the young father was as scared and helpless as they were. Birth fathers could be a bit removed from the pregnancy, but the birth mothers had to deal with it for nine months and then all its ramifications afterward.

Many birth mothers still hold some anger toward their own parents since in most cases the parents were the ones who made all the arrangements during the pregnancy and subsequent adoption. Birth mothers also said they were still angry at other family members who, at the time, could have stepped in and taken their baby, thus keeping the child within their family.

If there was a successful reunion, the birth mothers appeared to be giddy with unbridled joy that their child made the effort to find them. Making up for the lost years was paramount to them, but they said they have to be careful not to intrude too much on their child's life. In many cases, the child feels the need to make up for lost time also, particularly at the beginning of this new relationship. Both parent and child say this new relationship is like that between two friends, not at all like parent and child. Both sides acknowledge that the child already has a set of parents, and that will never change. The birth parent is traditionally called by their first name, not Mother or Father. However, usually grandchildren do call the parents of their birth parents the traditional grandma or grandpa.

Most birth mothers say they have lived with their "shameful secret" all their lives. Most said their unplanned pregnancy was never spoken of again by their parents. This was a sad fact for them. It minimized the fact they had given birth to a child. Often, their younger siblings did not know of the birth because the birth mother was sent away somewhere until the baby was born. Often, too, even close relatives did not know because of the shame involved. This burden of being outside of society's norms was a constant companion for some women. Many did not marry after this experience, and some married "any man who would have me" because they were told by their parents and those who tended to them during their pregnancy that they were now "damaged goods."

One of the greatest benefits of a reunion is that this shame, strong and constant as it was, disappeared after meeting their birth child. These women dreaded the anger their birth child might have toward them, and usually there was no anger. Their children, now adults, could understand reasons why a young girl could not successfully raise a child alone. After seeing this attitude, these women were now free of this bondage that affected their self-esteem for so long.

One does hear in the adoption world the statement "If she had loved me, she would have found a way." This is often heard by a struggling adoptee in their teens or in their twenties. With more maturity and some objectivity, and an understanding of the times when shame was attached to birth out of wedlock, many do understand. These adoptees are grateful their birth mothers did not have an abortion.

A reunion does not end secrets; it can create more. Some birth parents and birth children are reunited, and the adoptive parents are not told. When there is physical distance between the adoptee and his adoptive parents, this secret is more easily kept. The adoptee fears his adoptive parents would be hurt or offended if they knew he was seeing his birth parent. Often the main relationship after a reunion between birth parent and child is by telephone or e-mail to make the secret tighter.

Resentment from the birth parent can surface here because they don't know the adoptive parents but hear about them from their child and feel cheated they are not recognized by the people who raised their common child. One secret is exposed, but another takes its place. The adopted child, now an adult, is placed in the middle trying to be the good child to both sets of parents. Some adoptees say this is exhausting and very stressful because keeping secrets is dangerous. They would rather do this, however, than face the perceived potential hurt feelings or ire of their adoptive parents.

Birth fathers may struggle with self-image issues when they realize in later years that they were responsible for bringing a human being into this world and then avoided all the consequences of that situation. They sometimes feel the responsibility in later years they did not feel as young men. If they try to search for their offspring, they often feel the adoptee may be angry at them for abandoning them as a baby as well as abandoning their birth mother.

It was evident in the interviews that both birth mothers and birth fathers still feel connected to their birth children. Whether they have a right to enter into their children's lives is considered debatable by them, but they still look upon their birth children as their children who were raised by other parents. Even when they say they don't want to be parents or replace their child's adoptive parents, the strong feeling is this: "I gave birth to that child, and that child will always be a part of me. The fact that other people raised him does not change the fact that he is my child."

Here are some birth-parent gains:

- Feeling of satisfaction knowing their child is being loved and raised by a family that truly wants a child, has probably been waiting a long time, and will value their child greatly.
- Knowledge that the adoptive family has been scrutinized by adoption professionals for safety, security, character, values, and economic means.
- If the birth mother is a teenager, she will be able to continue her education and job training without being fettered by the responsibility of caring for and raising a baby. Due to her young age, she probably does not yet possess these skills.
- If the birth father is a teenager, he may feel guilt that he is responsible for the birth mother going through pregnancy at too young an age. The knowledge that their baby will be raised by competent, more mature parents relieves him of responsibility for the child.

During the years after an adoption is legally completed, all sides of the triad experience joys and challenges caused by the adoption. It's generally thought that the birth parents have the most to lose. Unfortunately, the young pregnant mothers were made to feel great shame up until the 1970s, 1980s, and even some years after that.

In our interviews, many of the birth mothers were sent to homes for unwed mothers run by religious organizations. Many stated they were treated like "fallen women" and were told over and over that they'd be lucky if any man would marry them now that they had committed such a sin. Sadly, this treatment had heavy effects on these women who were young girls at the time. They said they carried their shame with them every day of their lives, often keeping it a secret from their eventual families.

It was interesting that if they searched for their birth child after thirty or forty years, they knew they had to tell their husbands about the existence of their first child. This they did reluctantly, but they were extremely apprehensive about telling their children that they had a half-sibling somewhere. Some even decided not to search after all because they couldn't bear to shame themselves in the eyes of their children. Those who did share this fact state that their children's reaction was surprisingly positive, even enthusiastic, that they had a half-sibling. Some even took over the search because their mother was doing it too slowly.

All the birth parents we interviewed said they were relieved once their secret was out and they were gratified at how well it was accepted. The era of great shame ended with their generation. Their current families, in general, thought it was not nearly as dire as the birth mother had believed for many years.

Even though an unplanned pregnancy was life changing for many young girls, they say they were consoled knowing their baby was in the arms of loving people and would grow up with opportunities for an education and experiences the birth mother could not provide.

The birth mother who relinquished her baby suffered a great loss. Those who were appreciative of the life they gave birth to and the life they arranged for their baby said they fared well in life. Because of their pregnancy and the ensuing complications and decisions, these girls had to grow up faster. They said the hardest part was living with the stigma of being part of an unplanned pregnancy. It didn't matter how many did or didn't know this fact. There were always some family members who knew.

Many went on to marry and establish loving families. A percentage larger than in the average population never married. Some we interviewed were still angry at the system in place when they had given birth that insisted a young unmarried woman could not raise a child. Those who were thankful their child was placed in a mature, loving home went on to develop a good life. They felt they were stronger people because of what they had to endure.

16

Adoptive-Parent Loss and Gain

Adoptees and birth parents often are not aware of adoptive-parent losses. They think adoptive parents come out the winners, but there is loss on all three sides.

The adoptive parents' losses include the following:

- Loss of their genetically linked offspring, a normal expectation since childhood
- Loss of biological family continuity, a break in generational continuance
- Loss of a sense of entitled parenting, society's view of them as substitute parents
- Loss of a sense of "This is my child forever," a fear of birth parents taking over
- Loss of parental security; "Will my adopted child wish he had been adopted by others?"
- Parenting in a very complicated state, having to deal with adoption issues as well as the regular parenting issues

- A more stressed family life, sometimes dealing with difficult genetic issues not of their own making, foreign to their family and requiring professional help
- Loss of a firm sense of family; loss of a sense of "We belong together no matter what because of blood ties"

Adoptive parents can diminish their sense of loss if they approach parenting their adopted child as parenting a unique individual instead of parenting their child as their own flesh and blood. Adoptive parenting is not often looked upon this way, however. Adoptive parents fold their child into their family bosom as if the child were born to them. They feel their love and devotion is as strong, if not stronger, than it would have been for any biological child born to them. As their child grows, a sense of loss can be exaggerated when their child develops into the child he was genetically engineered to become. This often is not the child the adoptive parents had in mind when they considered adoption. They are reminded of their loss when they see these differences and make a comparison to the fantasy of what their perceived mirror image biological children would be like.

Many adoptive parents think they can develop their child into what their genetic child might have been. Disappointment and frustration can be found along this path. Nature versus nurture comes into play, and in recent years, nature has been found to have a much greater influence than believed in years past. Some young parents don't want to hear from older adoptive parents who have been through this experience, but in recent years, more young adoptive parents are indeed realizing this fact to be true.

The beauty and joy of adoption can be found in families that look upon their adopted offspring as unique and individual, as human beings full of their own potential. Where there is an acceptance of the individuality of the child instead of an effort to mold the child into the family image, the adoption journey can be filled with satisfaction and accomplishment. It can be a joyful journey, indeed.

If the traditional "Take him and make him your own" philosophy is taken, the losses can be felt deeply for years. The first ten or so years of a child's life are not much different within the family whether a child is adopted or not. However, when adolescence takes over, many of the genetic propensities intensify. These are the years where both child and parent become aware of the many ways that the child differs from other family members. The "I don't fit" syndrome can intensify. This becomes stronger if there is pressure to fit in rather than pressure to be the very best person you were put on this earth to become. Each individual should be respected for whatever gifts and talents they bring with them into this world.

Many adoptees say that they went through their childhood acting so they would appear to be more like their adoptive families. They felt pressure to be like everyone else in the family, all the while feeling very different. In our interviews, too many adoptees said they really had a hard time figuring out who they truly were because they didn't want to be different from all the people around them. Another result of this pressure to be like other family members is outright rebellion and leaving the home and family prematurely.

It is difficult to tell adoptive parents who have longed for children, sometimes for years, that they should look upon their child as unique and not as their genetic offspring. They have longed for children for so long that the thought of any child not being fully their own in every sense is foreign to them. It is obvious that the feeling of loss here can be great.

When people fall in love and marry, our society expects the next step to be starting a family, one where the children are the biological offspring of the parents. Virtually all couples share in this cultural expectation. Couples who explore adoption opportunities are too often looking for children who would be as their biological children would be. Even couples who say they are "color-blind" and adopt a child of a different race often don't realize the uniqueness and individuality issues, which are multiplied by cultural factors.

The executive director of an adoption agency that deals with transracial adoptions says the one statement that still makes her cringe is when a potential adoptive parent says, "Oh, we're color-blind. Color and race make no difference to us." This woman says she then retorts, "Color and race may not make a difference to you, but it will make a difference to your child, and you need to understand and deal with this."

The fervency of adoptive parenting can make it difficult for adoptive parents to stand back to get a broader, objective perspective of the adoptive family. The definition of an adoptive family is when a couple (sometimes a single person) makes the commitment to raise and forever love a child from a different genetic background than their own. This can introduce many more issues into a family, and this fact is often glossed over by eager parents who can't wait to hug and love forever a baby or child. Many adoption professionals say they try to introduce realism into the adoptive family by saying there may be more challenges down the road than if they had given birth to their children. The professionals say over and over that adoptive parents don't want to hear it, and even if they believe it, they think they are the one family to beat the odds and all will go smoothly. They think they will incorporate their child into their family with no trouble at all because their love will be so strong.

This attitude, as prevalent as it is, can be the forerunner of disappointment and can make the losses feel even more painful when they realize their adopted child is not like how their fantasized biological child might be. Sadly, in this day of prevalent drug use, learning disorders and physical disorders can develop. Some of these are not obvious at the time of adoption and develop later, often to the surprise of the adoptive parents. A lot of effort and money for professional help can be expended if this is the case. Again, parents may think that their biological offspring would not have presented such challenges. The loss of a smoother family life can be felt during these times.

The losses are factual if one cannot produce a biological child. Adoption should not be a substitute to remedy this situation. Adoption should be an opportunity for a family to embrace an adopted child and look upon that child as an unfolding mystery. There is no road map or set of directions that accompany the child into the family. Any background information is usually what someone wants the adoptive family to hear, and it can include partial truths as well as important omissions.

Anyone who takes the plunge into adoption should see this as an unusual opportunity to love and nurture a unique individual. The unfolding of the baby into a child and eventually into an adult can be a wondrous journey if the adoptee is respected for who he is. His own talents and gifts need to be nurtured by his adoptive parents even though they are outside the experience of his adoptive family. A great sense of accomplishment can be gleamed by approaching adoption with this realistic approach. To help any person grow and develop into the best and most accomplished person their abilities allow should be the joyful goal of adoptive parents.

Often, this turns out to be other than what parents expected. In one case, a family adopted both a daughter and a son. Their daughter turned out to be about as perfect as any one person could be. Their son, unknown to them at the time of adoption, was the result of a rape. Years later, they found out the birth father was a psychopath, in prison for murder. After years of heartache and tears, and thousands spent on therapy, they came to the conclusion that one of their roles in life was to take this young man from childhood to adulthood in the best fashion they could. They provided him with years of counseling and opportunities for an education. The results were not what they had hoped for, but their attitude was they kept their son safe and out of trouble for the years he was in their home. They were of the generation that believed in the saying "Take him and make him your own." They struggled with this for years and felt they must be doing something wrong. Now they realize they did a wonderful job in providing their son a loving home.

The complications of adoption issues sometimes appear to be either right there in the middle of the room or, at best, sitting on a shelf nearby, waiting to get into the family action. Adoptive families are different from biological families. Adoptive families can be more challenging, but because of the opportunity for being more diverse, life can be more exciting because adopted children can lead their families into uncharted waters, outside of the traditional and genetic experiences parents are accustomed to. With an adventurous attitude and a lot of faith in your parenting, this can be quite a journey, one that biological parents truly cannot experience or understand. It can broaden and deepen your experience so that your perspective on life changes forever – for the better!

When asked, almost all adoptive parents said they would not go back (if given the chance) and replace their adopted children with their hypothetical biological children. We heard many stories of extremely difficult and disruptive lifestyles in adoptive families, but every adoptive parent in our interviews, including those with dramatically rebellious children, said adoption changed who they were. They talked about loving a child from another realm almost in a sacred sense. They did not know this from the beginning, but as life unfolded, they sensed what they were doing. They thought of themselves as being honored to be given a sacred responsibility, and they would never want to undo the effect adoption had on their family.

The adoptive-parent gains include the following:

- Being able to have a full family life they could not otherwise have
- By accepting "another woman's child," they automatically broaden their perspective on accepting and even embracing other people.
- They often feel they are the "chosen ones" instead of their child being the "chosen child." They can be chosen by the birth mother from several offerings given her—or by the

adoption agency—or they can feel life, destiny, or God chose them to parent their particular child.
- They can embrace a gratitude not experienced by biological parents because there was always a chance their child might have been placed in another family instead of theirs. An extraordinary appreciation of their child comes from this realization.
- Because their adopted child comes from a different genetic background, the adoptive family often experiences personalities, talents, and phenomena further away from the comfort of their own gene pool. This can be difficult, but it can also be stimulating by forcing parents to adjust to a broader spectrum of life than they might otherwise have had. Because of this concept, adoptive parents say they grow into better people.

At the end of each interview with adoptive parents, we asked, "Knowing what you know now, if you had to do it all over again, would you adopt?" In many interviews, it seemed obvious that after relating all the drama and sorrow that their family went through, some adoptive parents would have said they regretted adopting. None of them ever did.

Each and every adoptive parent, some relating tragic circumstances, all said enthusiastically and without hesitation, "Of course, we'd adopt again. No one could understand our child better than we do. No one could have a stronger love for our child than we do. And the benefit of all we've gone through is that we are all better people for showing that our love helped our child cope and adjust. It may not have been perfect, and I'm sure we made mistakes, but no one can say we're not a family that loves each other."

Adoptive parents say they really had to stretch during the years to accept some behaviors and differences they weren't comfortable with at the beginning. Some say they tried to mold their child into a child who would have been born to them. Others looked at their child as a unique gift from life and nurtured their child, differences and all. No matter what tactic the parents took, they all said they were forced to grow into an acceptance of humanity in general they wouldn't have experienced were it not for adoption. They felt this made them better people—perhaps not at the beginning, but eventually, it made them better, more loving parents.

Gratitude was often expressed in the interviews. Many adoptive parents said they were young and living a rather programmed life before they adopted. Adoption and its ensuing issues forced them out of their comfort zone. This produced an understanding tolerance they didn't possess before.

Adoptive parents also expressed gratitude toward the birth parents, known or unknown. Anyone who loves a child knows it is unthinkable to not have that child in your life. In every adoption, there is only one child but two sets of parents. One set has the child, and the other doesn't. This is not lost on the adoptive parents.

Adoptive parents are chosen by some person to parent a child: the adoption agency, a private doctor or lawyer, or the birth parent. In any decision made, there are alternatives and factors that go into the decision. Often it's a small factor. One birth mother said she chose a particular family because they had two dogs and she liked dogs and wanted her child to grow up with dogs.

The fact that some other family might possibly have "their child" if another decision had been made is a frightening thought to adoptive parents but also one that makes them thankful they were the ones chosen. It often makes them feel they want to hold their child tightly in every sense. Parents in a biological family don't experience this because no one else could possibly be the parent of their child because their child was born to them.

Every prospective parent has idealistic thoughts about their future children. They dream about how close they'll be in shared interests and activities. They don't anticipate the challenges that over the years all parents face. Life often takes parents on journeys they aren't prepared for, some very difficult. A very wise mother of seven, who had been a mother for many years, was heard to say, "Children don't necessarily make your life happy. Children make your life full."

That's a statement many can relate to. Both adoptive parents and biological parents have their lives changed by raising children. Adoptive parents, because they feel they've been stretched further than biological parents, feel that in the end their lives are blessed because they've been forced to become deeper, more tolerant, and more understanding people. Their sense of gratitude toward birth parents and life in general is something they feel deeply and express often.

17

Adoptive Families

I heard one social worker who had worked in the adoption field for over thirty years say recently, "I can't believe what we did to these families all these years. We had no idea what we were getting them into. We handed them a baby and then sent them naively on their way." Adoptive families have struggled for years thinking they should be just like biological families. They are not.

The anger felt by adoptees at not being kept by their birth mothers, the anger felt by birth mothers who gave birth in a society that would only let them keep their babies by experiencing great shame and disgrace, and the bewilderment by adoptive parents who didn't understand why their child was so angry and didn't feel he fit in – for years, these issues were never addressed in our society. When any one in the triad brought up these issues, they were dismissed by those listening as not unique or important. People involved felt alone and misunderstood.

There are many similarities between biological families and adoptive families, of course, but there are some unique differences also as we now acknowledge. These can be seen quite clearly after the children are grown and one can look back upon the experience.

In adoptive families where all has gone well, the parents seem ebullient, and even relieved, that all has gone well. They realize in later years something they were not aware of at the time of adoption: that they were to love and raise children quite different from themselves and that these differences could be a very big factor. Several decades ago, adoptive parents were told, "Forget your child is adopted. Just raise him as your own."

Even if there was a bit of apprehension about adoption, these parents *knew* their love could conquer all. Since international and transracial adoption became more common and there were obvious physical differences between parents and children, these parents also knew their love could conquer all problems and they would have a happy and successful family. Where there was success, these adoptive parents appear even more pleased than biological parents with successful grown children because adoptive parents now see many adoptive families around them that do not enjoy the same positive result. They almost feel they had the "luck of the draw" with their children as they realize that other adoptive families with parents just as loving and wise as they were didn't fare as well.

Adoptive families who have experienced serious problems differ from biological families with the same difficulties. In biological families where there are learning disabilities, addiction problems, antisocial behavior, etc., usually there is some obvious or insinuated incidence of the same or similar problem among some other family member. There may have been experience within the family with the same often-inherited issue. When symptoms of a problem surface, the biological family may see some similarity to Uncle Joe or Cousin Mary and be able to address the issue directly. They know what they may be dealing with. At least, it's a place for them to start.

In adoptive families where a problem is surfacing, often the adoptive parents have had no exposure to the individual issue their child is dealing with. They don't recognize symptoms as symptoms. They often don't want to see a problem or wonder if this is just the personality of their child, knowing their child comes from a different gene pool than their families. They can question their parenting skills during this time, wondering if they have done something wrong to make their child act in a different way.

When professional help is sought, there is often little or no biological background knowledge for the professional to start with. He is dealing with a child with symptoms but has little or no genetic information to guide him. It is often at this point that the adoptive family goes back to the adoption agency to plead for more information about their child's background. In situations like this, biological information can be very helpful. Sometimes it is available, sometimes it is not. There are many stories of families going through years of counseling only to find out after their child is an adult that as a child he was treated for the wrong issue.

Attention deficit disorder was widely given as the reason for some children's problems. Now anxiety disorder has been found to be the correct diagnosis in many cases of adopted children, not ADD. Research has shown that a baby taken from its birth mother can suffer trauma and anxiety. Many adoptive parents have spoken over the years of the general anger they saw and couldn't understand in their child. When given the description of anxiety disorder, many see it was a general anxiety and "unsettledness" in their child that could have prompted frustration and anger.

Many adult adoptees now say that they went to psychiatrists for years and were medicated for years, only to realize as adults that their issues were not depression, addictions, etc., but, in fact, grief issues over their lost original family. No one ever helped them grieve for their loss, but it played out in antisocial behavior during their childhood, and no adult around them understood why.

In some adoptive families, at the time when they went back to the adoption agency to find out information that could help their child, they were shocked at what they were told. At the time of the adoption, these parents were told the good things, but detrimental items often were not shared. By the time their child is an adolescent, the family may have already spent years in confusion and frustration because of their child's disruptive behavior that they cannot account for. Once the background information is learned, then the pieces of the puzzle may fall into place. This can help parents, as well as the professional, in helping their child.

In extreme cases, when new background details are learned, adoptive parents can become very angry. This is where they differ from biological families with serious issues. First of all, the adoptive parents are angry they were never told (if the adoption agency knew), and secondly, their own infertility issues can resurface. One logical thought would be "If only we'd been able to have biological children, we wouldn't be facing this nightmare now."

The ideal solution to this is to have adoptive parents as informed as biological parents as to the history of their children. With some present adoptions, particularly some international adoptions, this is not possible. Even in open adoptions where the birth mother and adoptive parents meet, the truth about detrimental background information can be withheld by the birth mother. She wants her baby placed in the best home possible and knows that if there is too much baggage attached to her baby, he may be hard to place.

There are many loving families of all kinds who stand by their troubled children. This appears to be what parents do. Some parents do reach their limit and say they can't do any more. They say they have done all they can. They are through. In adoptive families, many parents at this juncture know their child has no biological family members to support him, so it is especially difficult for them to throw in the towel, so to speak. In biological families, there may be an older sibling or relative who sympathizes with the person exhibiting negative behavior, and that person can take over the caretaker role. In adoptive families, this can happen, but often there is an issue of "What else don't we know about this person? What else is in his gene structure that may play out?" There can be more reticence to get involved because of the unknown background. They think they may be getting into a situation they can't handle. Adoptive relatives also can look at the adoptive parents and say, "They've been wonderful, loving parents. If they can't handle him, what makes me think I can help him?"

In adoptive families, as in biological families, often "staying power" pays off. If an adoptee had problems as a child and an adolescent and a teenager, he—often in his thirties or forties—will have a perspective that makes his issues clear to him. Many adoptees live for years managing issues as best they can, but as they mature, they have a keener sense of themselves.

Many adult adoptees say their key issues are those of trust and abandonment. They are now happy, well-adjusted adults, but looking back, they see the logic of why they felt the way they did. It now makes sense to them. They felt abandoned by their original family and, because of this, wondered how safe it was to trust others in their lives.

Adoptive families should know this now. Years ago, there was little information to share about adoptees' feelings and issues, but now we know more. Adoption was not an issue for the adoptive parents who loved their children, and they couldn't imagine that adoption was an issue for their strongly loved children. Children had a hard time expressing it in a logical verbal way, so at times, they acted out. Families currently adopting children now have the advantage of past years successes and failures. We've learned more from the failures. Our adopted children do have to be told that we are families forever, that we love our adopted children and they can trust us to be there always.

In years past, adoptive parents knew this and assumed their children knew this too. If a child is told this verbally on a regular basis, he won't have to act out and test his parents to see when his adoptive parents will "give him away," just like his biological parents did. More than one adoptive parent has been told by their adopted (now adult) child, "I don't know why you didn't throw me out. I kept raising the bar doing worse and worse things to prove to myself that I was a throwaway. You sure put up with an awful lot."

In the interviews for this book, the staying power of adoptive families was proven to us. Their love for their child was steady—tested many times, but always steady. Sometimes the child didn't trust that love. Often these parents did not know what was going on in their child's head. They didn't realize that their child was scared because he felt he wasn't loved like a biological child would be loved, that his position in the family was not as secure as a biological child's would be, and that he might not be all that his adoptive parents hoped for in a child.

In years past, adoptive parents were in the dark about all these issues. In many families, their love surely did not conquer all, but their steady love took them through some very painful years, and they felt right in maintaining that love. They might have been baffled as to their child's behavior, but they knew they loved their child. Years ago, adoption help wasn't available to these families as it is today. Adoption issues were neglected and dismissed.

Now in this enlightened time, adoptive families have knowledge available to them to support them. Sadly, much of this knowledge comes from the pain of adoptions in the past. We need to be grateful that this knowledge is now talked about and written about, and we should acknowledge the families in the past who were put into a situation where they were given no information or false information. It's amazing some of them did as well as they did.

Society often looks at adoptive parents and adoptees with judgment. Most adoptees, who are now adults, grew up with very little information to validate their feelings. The fortunate ones had loving families, but they were also groping in the dark, wanting desperately to help but didn't have the knowledge to identify the problems as adoption issues. The solace for these families is that they did all they could for their adopted children. Society wasn't ready to explore the consequences that adoption had on some children. We've come a long way but still have a much longer road ahead. Adoptees and their families who traveled the adoption road with no map should be very proud of how well they did with no direction. If there were painful years, they didn't feel very good at the time, but now, with perspective, they know they did the best they could, and it's probably safe to say they did a very good job.

For those who have thought there is no adoption effect, I hope the stories in this book have helped them to realize that every aspect of our life has an effect one way or the other. Being adopted, relinquishing a child, or raising an adopted child with adoption issues certainly has an effect on lives. It's not just the immediate people involved that live with the effect; it's their families as well.

People know even before they become parents that if they raise a child, they will be a strong influence on that child. What parents often don't realize is that their child will also be a strong influence on them. Parents help children grow, but children also help parents grow.

We're never through changing, developing, and growing. Joy and satisfaction should be the goal for both parent and child as together they embark on this journey we call life. What we do is important, and who we are is very important. Most people interviewed recognized that they are a far better person now—all because their lives were touched by adoption.

18

Perspective

Millions of people around the world are touched by adoption. The concept of adoption, a child being raised by a family other than the one he was born into, has been around since mankind began. A child can be separated from his birth family because of the death of a family member, societal norms, or any other number of circumstances. In the past, as well as now, there is usually another family longing to parent that child. That's the nature of mankind. Adults protect, care for, and love children. If you take a child who cannot be raised by his birth family into your family, that's called adoption.

The concept of adoption touching your life is rarely something you plan ahead for. There are many circumstances prohibiting birth parents from parenting their child. Usually, these situations are not sought after; they just happen. It's called life.

In an anthropology course in college I recall reading about a primitive tribe in Africa that established a system where everyone was adopted. Members of the tribe in their late teens and twenties bore babies who were then placed with tribal couples in their thirties and forties. Undoubtedly, the tribal elders thought that older parents could provide better parenting skills than those who physically bore the babies. The message was nature may make the young human body capable of bearing a child, but older tribal members would have more mature parenting skills. I remember being very surprised at this concept, but one can see some sense of order to it.

Adoption today is filled with laws, regulations, paperwork, agonizingly long periods of waiting, frustrations, heartache, personal dilemmas, choices, and finally decisions. Those of us personally touched by adoption know adoption today is also filled with anticipation, joy, fulfillment, and love. We all do the best we can. The system may not be perfect, and we all know people aren't perfect, but we are not unlike people who for centuries have tried to do the best they can for a child who, for whatever reason, could not be parented by the people who brought him into this world.

It takes a unique ability to understand and graciously accept the concept of adoption. It isn't an easy road, and we have many choices all along that road. We can be bitter and resentful, or we can see our roles as part of the long history of many different kinds of adoption throughout the ages.

The process of adoption starts with loss: the loss of a probable biological acceptance and love. The process of adoption ends with embracing acceptance and love from another source. For adoption to be successful, both the loss of a biological love and the offer of a new love need to be accepted. Both of these aspects need to be, not just accepted, but absorbed and embraced. As human beings, we need to appreciate love where it is offered. It may take years of struggle, but most of those we interviewed found they were happier not dwelling on the past where love was lost but instead living in the present where love surrounded them.

Some we interviewed still felt some bitterness and resentment, but most said that being touched by adoption changed them forever, and they would never want to undo that part of their lives. They realized they were part of a special human phenomenon, and they felt they were given the opportunity to be part of a human practice where a family love is not constrained to just those we are physically related to. Our interviewees were a small link in an ongoing large chain of families who have lived a larger love, an expanded love, which included loving a small, little stranger placed in their family.

Years ago when my husband and I were newlyweds, we went to a movie that addressed adoption in its very natural state. The movie was a true story about an Indiana pioneer family in the 1800s where both parents died leaving behind six young children. They lived in a small pioneer settlement, and other families offered to take in the orphaned children. The oldest, a sixteen-year-old boy, agreed with all the younger children that they could manage by themselves and stay in the family cabin. Reality set in after several months, and the oldest son realized he could not care for all the children.

The last scene in the movie took place on a dark, snowy Christmas Eve. The sixteen-year-old boy took his younger siblings one by one out through the deep snow to a neighbor's cabin. Each child carried a small bundle containing his worldly possessions. The oldest son knocked on each door and asked if his younger brother or sister could live with that family. The townspeople had wanted to take in the orphans all along, and each child was placed with a family that wanted them.

The scene on the screen was poignant—the night darkness, the deep snow, the only light and warmth coming to the screen came as each cabin door opened revealing a room filled with inviting light from the fireplace and kerosene lamps and warmth and love shown by the accepting family. I wouldn't be surprised if "Silent Night" was the background music for this long emotional scene.

There wasn't a dry eye in the theater, including my husband's. That was the first time I had ever seen tears in his eyes, the kind you had to wipe away. He talked about that movie for years afterward. The audience was drawn into the experience, feeling both the pain of loss and the security coming from an offer of love. What we saw was adoption, the simple kind that the human race has embraced for centuries.

The stories chronicled in this book are about people who are part of a continuation of that tradition. Each story is unique. Each had a different set of circumstances, and each accepted their experience and its ramifications in their own way. Some were more successful than others. Many looked upon this as an opportunity and considered it a gift life offered them. They had not planned on it, but those whose perspective allowed them to see their experience within adoption as an insight into embracing a more expansive kind of love were grateful. Grateful, indeed.